Conversations with the Horse

The official book of the award-winning 'Listening to the Horse' documentary, created by Irish horsewoman & film-maker, Elaine Heney.

By Elaine Heney

Conversations with the Horse

Published by Grey Pony Films

www.greyponyfilms.com

Meet Elaine Heney

Elaine Heney is an Irish horsewoman, film producer at Grey Pony Films, #1 best-selling author, and director of the award-winning 'Listening to the Horse™' documentary. She has helped over 120,000+ horse owners in 113 countries to create wonderful relationships with their horses. She lives in Ireland with her horses Ozzie & Matilda.

Fancy a movie night?

Listening to the Horse is the docu-series created by Elaine Heney. This 7 part award-winning documentary features over 70+ of the world's most inspiring horse people including Mark Rashid, Jim Masterson, Dr. Robert Miller, Jeff Sanders, Steve Halfpenny, Eitan Beth-Halachmy, Lester Buckley, Smokie Brannaman, Elaine Heney, Carolyn Resnick, Warwick Schiller, Guy McLean, Kim Walnes, Dagmar, Julie Goodnight, Karen Rohlf and many more.

Watch episode 1 today.

GET YOUR FREE MOVIE TICKET:

www.listentothehorse.com

Table of Contents

Foreword with Elaine Heney	9
The try and the release	12
The story of a mounted police officer	16
Is your name Chester?	24
Can dressage horses be light and soft?	30
Too old to be a good rider?	33
Looking for a retirement home	37
How do you think the horse feels about that?	41
Helping Baz to find his try	45
Could I have been the problem?	50
Are you asking your horse to go away?	55
Going back to basics	57
Could it be due to pain?	62
Miniature horse adventures	65
Listening to Pete	69
The power of the bladder meridian technique	73
One step at a time	77
My name is Lucy	80
Are they lonely?	83
Considering your horse's health	86
Have faith in yourself	89
Every horse matters	97
Stabling and health	100
A 15 year old experiments	104
Horses understand more than you realize	107
Lengthen your lower back	110
Softness, patience and lightness	113
Lessons learned	115
Inspiration with Jim, Jeff and Lester	122
Final thoughts from Elaine	125

Foreword

I started riding aged 6, with the purchase of my first Shetland pony called Breezly. We soon became inseparable. Even though he didn't move any faster than a walk (he was very economically minded), that was perfect for me. And we spent a lot of time together as great friends.

My fascination with horses was influenced by my Dad. When I was about eight years old, he bought a young horse and over the next three or four years, he would slowly back the horse, then start riding it in the fields, and then take it schooling over the Irish ditches & banks we are famous for.

I remember watching this process at a young age, and comparing it to magic. It looks like something magical, to be able to change a young, inexperienced horse, to a calm, friendly, beautiful mannered riding horse.

From age six the principals I still believe today were put in place. You are always patient with a horse. You always give the horse time to figure things out. You work on things in small incremental steps, and build confidence and relaxation along the way. You never hit a horse, or use aggression. A horse is to be treated with respect and kindness.

As I grew older I saw other people who didn't quite agree with these principals, so in my late teens and early twenties, I withdrew from competitions and 'advanced lessons', because they didn't align with what my Dad taught me when I was six years old.

After my first job in an office in Dublin, I went back-packing in New Zealand and I found an inspiring horse treks in the Southern Alps. Not only did they share my principals to do no harm, but they rode their horses doing really advanced moves with relaxation, softness and lightness.

My life changed totally. Now I could see what was possible. Since then, I've continued to be fascinated by good horsemanship.

After many years of hosting clinics & travelling around the world, I found myself behind a camera on set with Steve Halfpenny, the renowned Australian horseman, working on my first short documentary. This led to my first feature length documentary 'Soft Feel & Light Horses', both of which won many films festival awards.

Soon after that, I began work on the Listening to the Horse docu-series. I invited over 70 of the world's most inspiring horse people to join me in this documentary.

After this documentary premiered online in 2018, to tens of thousands of horse owners, I started to get emails from people all around the world, from the USA & Canada, Europe, to South Africa, Asia, Australia & New Zealand.

In these emails I read the most amazing stories of the lessons they learned from the Listening to the Horse docu-series.

Because these stories were so powerful, I knew they needed to be shared with the world.

This book is the result.

I want to thank everyone who watched the documentary, and a special thanks to those who submitted their stories.

It's my honor and privilege to call you my friends.

Elaine Heney

www.greyponyfilms.com

The try and the release

I have been riding horses for 22 years now and I have owned and cared for horses for 18 years. I have loved horses since the moment my uncle sat me on a pony at the local riding school at the age of 6.

My involvement with horses has morphed and changed over the years. I have gone from the pure adoration of a child to frustration with learning how to ride, riding out racehorses, hunting, starting young horses. I have been through the make the horse do your bidding with a big stick if necessary phase, which I am not so proud of.

When I started breaking young horses I had not had a whole lot of instruction in the matter so I tend to do it in a manner that makes the most sense to me with the least amount of fuss and gadgets possible. In the last few years I have been involved retraining abused ponies which has forced me to research all manner of equine behaviour, natural horsemanship techniques, neuroscience and more esoteric stuff also. I have trained as a craniosacral therapist for both humans and horses.

During the course of this work I have witnessed horses voluntarily involving themselves in helping people to heal trauma and release physical and emotional restrictions. I have witnessed my own horses, who had no previous experience of this type of work barring the craniosacral therapy treatments I have given them, help severely disabled children and their families with their healing process. Because of this I have returned to that sense of awe that I felt for them as a child. They are far more intelligent than we give them credit for. We owe it to them to the best we can to understand them and help them understand what it is we are asking of them and to quote Mark Rashid give them our Whole Heart when we work with them.

I have also learned over the years that there are horses of many different sensitivity levels and some of the most 'difficult' horses need us to deal with our own emotional baggage and approach them with a clear head in order to be able to work with us. We also need to develop our own level of sensitivity to what the horse is trying to communicate.

I recently watched 'Listening to the Horse' docu-series. After watching episode 2 of the series I think it was, I decided to try some pressure and release with a six month old thoroughbred foal that I had been working with. 'Buddy' had very little handling up until he was taken in and weaned in preparation for the upcoming foal sales. My job was to teach him general handling, catching and leading at a walk and a trot. Buddy found weaning quite stressful and was properly angry at people for a good 2 weeks after his mammy was taken away from him – ears back, biting when handled. Once he got over all of this I started working in earnest on catching and haltering him.

After a couple of days in the stable teaching him to respond to me pulling on the rope and stopping, turning etc. it was time to lead him out to the arena to run off some steam. Apart from being lively having been indoors for a couple of weeks he was pretty good that first day out. The biggest problem I had was stopping him once he was moving and having him walk over me when I stopped. I have to say I was previously sold on the idea of pressure and release and use it regularly in handling and training my horses but it's always nice to have a little reminder of how to do these things in practice.

After watching the second episode of Listening to the Horse I was working with Buddy in the arena when the idea popped into my head that I could teach him to back up and that would help with his stopping problem.

So I started by putting pressure on the lead rope, no response. So I got heavier with my pressure with still no response. I pushed him from the chest.... Nothing. Hmmmmm........ Why was this not working?

And then it occurred to me, was I pushing so hard that I wasn't feeling his response? So I started again with a light pressure on the rope. As soon as felt Buddy's weight shift back I released the rope immediately and told him he was brilliant. The second time he shifted his weight further back and I released the rope immediately. The third time he took a step back with the lightest touch on the rope and gave him lots of praise.

We walked around the arena a little bit after this to give Buddy time to mull over what we had just done. Roughly 5 minutes in Buddy had learned to walk forward when I walked forward, stop when I stopped and back up when I backed up. All this from lightening up on the pressure I was using and rewarding his trying to find the answer to the question I was asking. What a clever boy! I do think that along with the timing of the release the genuine feeling of gratitude and happiness at his responses that he felt from me has made training him very easy. Buddy is now walking and trotting beautifully along by my side at whatever pace I set off my voice and energy and doesn't hesitate to follow me anywhere.

Lisa Fitzgerald

The story of a mounted police officer

My name is Claire Bloomfield and I am 57 years old. My sister and I have always loved horses since childhood, but were never lucky enough to have our own. We used to work at a local stables so that we could ride horses in return. In 1980, I joined the Metropolitan Police and had a challenging career as Mounted Police Officer, which unfortunately had the effect of almost putting me off horses for life.

My first Police horse was a three year old thoroughbred that had already been raced! I left the Police force in 1996, and up until 2013 I had barely any contact with horses. I also had three boys, one of whom has learning difficulties, so I had no time to even consider getting back with horses. I went on to develop breast cancer in 2010. However, after a successful course of treatment I have put that behind me and now live my life to the fullest.

Luckily I had the opportunity to go on a holiday to Costa Rica with my brother in 2013. I enquired about horse riding and somebody recommended a horse ranch near to where we were staying.

We went for a two hour ride on American Quarter Horses, which we were remarkably well behaved. Even though my brother couldn't ride, he was able to manage without being on a lead rein and even coped with going for a short canter! Whilst we were waiting at the airport coming home, I kept talking about the horses and how wonderful they were, so my brother then said, 'You only live once, life is short and you obviously still love horses so why don't you get one?'

The rest, as they say, is history! For the last five years I have been in partnership with a beautiful red dun American Quarter Horse, called Ronnie. He has been my greatest teacher and has filled my life with a pleasure that I could only ever have imagined.

I took Ronnie on just before he turned four, and he had a bit of a history. He was a bit too much horse for his owner and used to buck people off. He then had a young man look after him, who rode him in a martingale and dropped noseband that Ronnie was never too happy about.

We started off at a dressage livery yard and moved a few times before settling at The Centre of Horseback Combat where we have been for over three years. We are both very happy there. Ronnie has been a challenging little horse, and I think that without my strong seat (through riding many challenging police horses) Ronnie could have ended up as a non ridden equine, or even have needed to have been rehomed.

For about the past four years we have been following a natural horsemanship programme which has enabled us to safely make a lot of progress. The lessons and clinics that I have attended have been invaluable as they have given me some understanding of horse and human psychology, as well as giving me the tools and techniques to deal with any horse situation.

All my years as a child, and also during my time in the Mounted Police, I was always confident around horses, but wasn't what you would call a horsewoman. Now a whole world of horsemanship has opened up in front of me, and I am loving every minute. Ronnie has come on in leaps and bounds. He is now ulcer free, is a good weight, has muscled up, is moving much better and canters without bucking! He has the best life that I can give him. He whinnies when I arrive at the yard and makes funny faces and noises!

One of our grooms commented this week that she has never seen a bond as strong as the bond between Ronnie and I, and she always knows from his behavior when I have turned up.

Since watching the Listening to the Horse videos I feel that I now have the stepping stone to progress my horsemanship much further. Everything that was discussed in the videos made complete sense to me.

Many of the contributors have inspired me to make some changes, particularly Steve Halfpenny and Jeff Sanders. (I had never heard of them before, but now have a rider's space on Steve's UK clinic in July and a place on Jeff's UK clinic next year, as well as a spectator's place in June this year.)

Steve has a calm demeanour and listening to him had made me rethink the way that I train Ronnie, especially with regards to whether or not I move my feet whilst training him from the ground. I have always been taught not to move my feet, but I believe that Steve was saying the opposite.

Alongside some of the other commentators he was saying that it is important not to pull on a horse, as you can only pull a horse towards you, not pull him away, which could cause the horse to become confused. I found that fascinating and have already made changes whilst practicing ground work with Ronnie.

Ronnie is currently ridden in either a rope head collar, rope hackamore or a lunge cavesson. This is because Ronnie objects to having a bit in his mouth.

This leads me on to the changes that I intend to bring in after listening to Jeff Sanders.

I didn't know anything about Californian Vaqueros until I watched the Listening to the Horse videos. Jeff explained how focusing on function that preserves the body of the horse and maintains relaxation, leads to the horse hopefully having a long and healthy life.

Jeff emphasised the importance of working a horse in collection in a relaxed way. He said that it was like taking a horse to the gym, by getting the horse's weight on the hind end and the need for bending the horse's joints in the hind end as they have more bend than the ones in the front. He also mentioned how the horse's withers drop with the weight of a rider, and the withers should be higher than the scapula. I have always found learning more about horse anatomy quite confusing, but Jeff's explanation of how the dorsal ligament can be overstretched by rollkur and forward down helped me to understand this much better. This is especially relevant for Quarter Horses, who are built downhill, which can be made worse by riding with the head too far down.

I found out from listening to Jeff, that the poll should not go below the height of the withers. Also helpful was hearing how our spine should be above the horse's 15th vertebrae and not further back (I hadn't realised that western saddles put the rider behind the strong part of the horse's back, which makes things harder for both the horse and rider, (although I had heard that western saddles don't distribute weight as efficiently as a standard English saddle.)

Also helpful to Ronnie and I, was learning the importance of fitting a hackamore in the right way, and if you are going to ride your horse in a bridle, which bits are most comfortable for the horse. Jeff explained where to have your hands while riding, i.e. not too high and not too low, and to push your horse rather than pull him.

After watching Jeff I have been lent a bosal and rope and have an expert coming out to help me fit this to Ronnie with the intention of riding him in an appropriate bridle eventually.

Other parts of the video I found particularly helpful were Lester Buckley explaining how he motivated a horse that wasn't already motivated to herd cattle. He told us how he rewarded the 'slightest try for the day' in order to get the desire out from the inside of the horse. This will be useful for training Ronnie as he can be quite introverted and nappy! Lester also suggested throwing your heart into a movement, rather than your head which I have already found helpful when asking Ronnie to canter under saddle.

Dr. Robert Miller reinforced the need to work slowly with your horse to prevent a fear reaction which interferes with the horse's learning. That is something that I need to remind myself of frequently, as I am quite a high energy, extroverted person!

Warwick Schiller talked about how a horse can tolerate scary things, but to be aware that the fear can build up after more exposure (even on one ride,) which can then lead to the horse exploding when his fear notches up to a level that he can no longer cope with.

This helped me understand how Ronnie can appear relaxed, but can get overwhelmed, which then initiates a fear or flight response. Warwick also said that we have often been told to never let a horse win, but he believes the opposite is true, i.e. That you should let them win and have an opinion, and let them tell you where they want to be the most.

He explained how he solved the problem of a horse that reared every time he was asked to move away from the gate, (which is something that I have experienced with Ronnie,) by encouraging the horse to walk small circles near the gate and then letting the reins go loose when the horse walked away. This technique is much more helpful than a confrontation.

Listening to David Mellor and Pat Parelli explaining about footfalls, and the importance of knowing where the horse's hind feet are, is something that I think about much more whilst training Ronnie from the ground or under saddle.

Finally, the last change I have made since watching the Listening to the Horse videos is that at the beginning of nearly every session with Ronnie, I follow Ronnie's bladder meridian line as demonstrated in episode four by Jim Masterton, which Ronnie seems to enjoy. We also end our sessions in the same way and often add in some stretching exercises, followed by a massage!

Ronnie and I have attended many clinics together. However, after watching the Listening to the Horse videos, we are now heading towards the Californian Vaquero style of riding as I feel that this is what Ronnie was made for. It has given us focus and I cannot wait to see where it leads.

A very big thank you Elaine for making these videos and letting us all receive such important information to help us listen to our horses more effectively, whilst keeping their best interests at heart and making the world a better place for them. *Claire Bloomfield.*

Is your name Chester?

Like most horse enthusiasts, I have loved horses and the very idea of horses since I was a young girl. I did not own many horses... only two until my most recent acquisition. I mostly rented horses or took lessons on other people's horses. I wasn't able to have many lessons. It was expensive and I would help pay for my two weeks of lessons each year by helping in the kitchen and cleaning the house of my teacher. I would have walked through hellfire to ride so I didn't mind any of that.

My parents had a car accident when I was 14 and that changed all our lives for the worse. Horses were no longer an option. I went on to pursue a career as a nurse and an interest in boys rather than horses.

I rode from time to time if the opportunity arose but then got married and had children. Work and accidents led to arthritis in my back. I rarely even thought of horses anymore.

Then one day my office mate, who started taking riding lessons at age 45, asked if I knew anyone who would like to go to a guest ranch. Well...yes! I would! But could I even ride still? I was 56! Would the arthritis prevent it?

We drove 700 km round trip to ride for one long weekend, half of which was rainy. But that weekend relit the fire, and was surprisingly good for my back! The kids were all grown up and gone. I wanted to ride again, but somewhere closer to home. My internet search found a guest ranch 1 hour west of my city. I was given a mare to ride with more whoa than go. Meanwhile a young woman riding with us was riding a fiery black and white Paint named Ricky. It was love at first sight for me. I asked if I could ride him next time.

Ricky was 18 when I started riding him. Although gelded, his early years were spent at stud, and he still saw himself that way. I spent the first year of our partnership just trying to catch him. Riding him took courage and was a complete thrill.

A year after I started riding him, the owner said they were going to sell him. I was the only person who could ride him besides the owner, which resulted in him being somewhat useless on a guest ranch. The plan was to send him to auction. Ricky had mild heaves. A 19 year old horse with heaves was unlikely to be adopted into a nice home. I went home and told my Husband that I thought I had to buy him.

Ricky was never an easy horse. He had one speed....fast. He had to be in front. He had to be the leader. He made me work for every bit of progress and trust. And it was only in the last year of his life that he came to me. I always had to go to him. But oh, how I loved him!

When Ricky died of colic at age 27, I was beyond devastated. When he died, we had been partnered for 9 years, 8 of which I was his owner. He died in my arms and I know he loved me as much as I loved him.

I am older....65. Not many women my age are active riders, so many of my friends are much younger than me. After a couple of months of mourning, I suddenly found myself receiving messages and emails containing pictures of horses. "What do you think of this one? He has a nice eye." "I picked up a really nice horse from BC. Maybe you would like to meet him." "I think this guy is really cute. What do you think?" I felt like I was participating in on-line dating, or starring on reality TV where the single girl chooses from a plethora of men. I knew what my friends were lovingly trying to do, but I wasn't that interested.

It was the eighth or so "offering" that really caught my attention. A dear friend sent me a video of a slightly worried looking chestnut with a forelock down to his nose who was penned with a weanling and a young palomino who was mistreated by the other horses. He was part of a herd that had essentially been hoarded, then abandoned. The people taking care of these horses had named him Hercules as he is so stocky and muscular. As I watched the video, the name "Chester" popped into my mind loud and clear.

By now I had watched your series and was so touched by every episode. Your movie had especially validated many of the animal communication beliefs I was increasingly holding. I decided to take a risk and asked my friend to suspend all judgment of my sanity, call the horse Chester and see what his reaction was. Another video popped into my messages. With the camera on him, my friend said "Chester?" Ears popped forward. "Is your name Chester?" He came to them. He had not done so during the first part of their visit.

My thought was, if a horse introduces himself to you, the least you can do is meet him. Two weeks later, he was mine.

At the time of this writing, it has only been a little over a week since Chester and I entered into our partnership, but the words "go slow" from the movie resonated strongly with me.

Chester is between 7 and 10 years old. His history is unknown. He is at least part Quarter horse. I have not pushed this young guy at all, but through small frequent exposures and successes, and through consistency, he is already amazing me every day with his own patience and rapidly developing trust. I started with just daily visits and sitting with him in his quarantine pen. I took him for walks in unfamiliar places. I talked to him. I fed him tasty grains. I groomed him. And I picked his feet, which is his fussy point. Unwilling to lift his feet, I needed to tap his ankle with the pick until he did, and then he would "bunch up", rather than relax into my hands. A little cookie and praise.

Day 2, quicker lifts, but tapping and bunching still happened. Cookie and much praise. Day 3, three out of four feet were lifted without tapping, but bunching still happened. Cookie and much praise. Day 4 all feet lifted without tapping, only hind legs bunched. Cookie and much, much praise!

Yesterday, I tried my tack on for fit. He was quite wonderful and patient as adjustments were made. Afterwards I put his rain sheet back on and as I was attaching each leg strap, up came that back foot! I had a good laugh and he got a hug and yes...a cookie and much praise! Going slow, lots of reinforcement and praise changed his behaviour with his feet in just 4 days! I finally rode him yesterday, just slowly up and down the arena fence line. I had bought him without even trying the ride. I definitely heard him "say" that my bitless bridle is too confusing for him, so next time we will try a bit. I know this is going to work as long as we take it slow.

I will always miss my first heart horse. But thanks to your movie, and the persistence of friends, I found the courage to open my heart again to another equine friend. "Go slow" and “listen to your horse” are phrases from the movie that I find are now ingrained in me. I am excited about using them as I embark on my journey with Chester. I know it will be a great one!

Doris Quinn

Can dressage horses be light and soft?

My name is Alex Boorman and I live in George, South Africa. I am a mom of 2 teenage boys. I have been working with horses since I was 12 years old and I am now 44. My riding career started when I taught myself to ride on the Shetland cross ponies at the local zoo where I did volunteer work. This was before I moved to George. I then progressed to working for lessons at a local yard, with an extremely good British riding instructor. This was where I received a fantastic riding foundation. In fact I have had the privilege of meeting and learning from many wonderful horse people along my journey. I have been teaching riding for 28 years.

Over the last 20 years I have been exploring ways of schooling and working with horses, that take the horse's welfare and thoughts into consideration, before the end goal.

This has meant moving away from the type of Dressage that we see a lot of today. In other words, no more tight nosebands, no more pulling the horse into a frame and kicking it up from behind and no more punishing the horse for misbehaving as their behavior is always caused by something we are doing.

Your 'Listening to the Horse' documentary was wonderful for me as it reaffirmed what I am doing and provided me with so many different perspectives on how to develop relationships with horses and have them want to work with us as partners. All the amazing horse people featured had so much wisdom to impart and it is so difficult to say who made the biggest impact on me, but I think I must mention Jeff Sanders.

Coming from a Dressage background, it was so refreshing to see how his way of schooling and working with horses produces such light, balanced and responsive horses without nervous tension. These are all things that are missing in most of the top Dressage horses we see today.

I have been interested in bitless riding for many years and I even backed my last horse with a bitless bridle as I actually feel safer that way. Listening to Jeff discuss how the horses are first taught everything in the bitless bridle or bosal, so that they respond to such subtle weight, rein and leg aids made so much sense. That way they are light and in balance before the bit is introduced, just for refinement. No pulling at all on the super sensitive mouth of the horse.

This just makes me so motivated to start my own horse this way!

In the meantime, I am taking my newfound enthusiasm and knowledge to all my pupils. I have one combination, Amy and King, who have made the transition to bitless riding. King is a different horse to ride, so much more relaxed over his back and he moves much more lightly and balanced. Amy is finding him so much more comfortable to ride too.

Another combination, Lizette and Ella, have come on so well. Ella was nervous and needed more confidence from her rider. This caused her to try and take control and she became dangerous to ride and handle.

We took a step back and Lizette worked on her confidence and consistency (both things spoken about many times in 'Listening to the Horse') and we basically started Ella from scratch. The two of them are now working beautifully together. These are just two examples. I am always excited to go to work to see the progress we can all make if we just consider the horse and continue to learn.

Alex Boorman

Too old to be a good rider?

To your question:" How this movie has influenced your way of listening to your horse" I have only one simple answer – CRYING!!!!

When I watched your movie I was crying in every episode. Silly old me you would say – yes I agree. Silly old me. As I could not believe this all is possible and true. Yes, now I know – silly old me.

I guess it was not only the film but the old pain I carried with me for several years. Thisguilt that I am not good enough and it's not possible for me. So here is my story. I can whisper – with a happy ending so far!

I am 35 year old horse lover from Latvia – small country (with less than 1.9 million people) in Europe. I started horse riding when I was about 12 years old – I took only a few lessons. Stables were out of the city and I had to use public transport to get there and back. At that time my parents had financial problems and when they asked me if I like my horse riding lessons – I said "no".

As for transport and lessons money was needed and I didn't want to ask for it. Kids understand more than parents tell them.

As you can imagine – my interest for horses didn't fade away. I took some random lessons in random stables in random years. Regular lessons I started to take when I was already 31. In summer time we had holidays from ballet lessons and I started to think – If I can do ballet, I could give a try for my childhood dream - horse riding. I was the oldest student there.

Beginning was hopeful but day by day my relationships with trainer got worse and worse and I could not handle how horses are treated there.

I still remember how little girl was punishing her horse for not taking the bridle, but it wasn't horse's fault. She did it really poorly. And those fears in horse's eyes – I still can see them. And yes – it was not the only time. And yes - it was accepted by trainer.

The last lesson with them was when we were out in the thunderstorm – she was sitting in her car with her friend. We were out in heavy rain and thunder. The only instructions I received was yelling that I am rubbish rider as I can't get my horse to move faster as she was just slowly walking. I was so scared as I didn't know how horses treat thunderstorms and I was scared from thunderstorm itself. I was sitting on the horse and crying. Only what I could do?

After that rough experience I took a few lessons more but left as my stress level was so high I could not remember lessons. Then tried another stables but the attitude was like – you are too old to be good rider, so we won't waste time to teach you. Some basics and off you go – walking in fields and that's all. It was already autumn and I went back to my ballet lessons.

I didn't try any more lessons as I concluded that it is my fault, I am poor rider, my dreams for horse riding are too high etc…

Our baby boy was born few years later and we changed big city life for small village far away. And there I noticed stables. I was passing several times till I gathered all my courage to ask for the visit. Small stables with 7 horses.

And here I am – still riding and doing it with joy.

The beginning was awful looking from physical point of you as I have had C-section with complications and a few months bed rest. It was like learning to walk again. I knew I could do it previously but was not possible at that time. Learning not to be harsh with myself. It has been almost a year with regular lessons and several falls now. And I took part in the first show. WoooooooW!!!

The biggest push for my dreams gave Katherine Chrisley Schreiber.

"The minimal amount of equipment, the minimal amount of things you can use, and the minimal severity of the equipment that you use will gain the best results, because you are working with the horse itself."

I was - and still am - amazed by riding the horse only with neck rope. And you know – I started to take lessons. Thank you Katherine for inspiring me and giving me the push that it's actually normal and nothing extreme if needed work is done.

Unfortunately the trainer for this riding is located far away and lessons can be taken really rarely – once per month or even one per 2 months. But... I have explained to myself - it's my patience's training. Not to rush into and take a deep breath. Believe me – it's not easy for me as I am quite fast in my temper.

I had a dream to own my own horse in 5 years time but now I am telling myself – I will own my own horse if I will be ready for it and when I will be really ready for it. I won't let anyone to influence me and will look for my horse with the greatest pedantism I can have in me. I want him/her to be part of my family and if purchased never sold.

Anete Koidu

Looking for a retirement home

After watching the docu-series “Listening to the Horse” I had some real, learning moments and a lot of ahhh yes I am doing it right moments.

One of the issues I am struggling with right now has to do with aging horses and death. Nothing makes me angrier than seeing ads on Facebook. “Looking for a retirement home for my 30 yr old mare. I have had her all her life, just need a place she can live out her last years”. Are you freaking kidding me!!! This horse has given you her life and her heart and now you want to re-home her to god knows where. Give her the love and respect she is due and allow her to die at home. Surrounded by her people, her herd and what she knows. Don’t just throw her away.

Unfortunately, my mare has severe osteoarthritis and we are just waiting for the day when she tells me she has had enough.

That the pain is too great. That she can no longer get up and down and can no longer be a horse. I am dreading that day.

Not only for me but also for her herd mates. Petunia has been with Duke since she was 7 years old and she is now 18. They have been separated for short periods of time but since we purchased them both they have been together 24/7 for the past 4 years. They are boss mare and first lieutenant of my little herd of 6. I believe, in my heart, that horses connect and develop deep relationships. I see it every day.

My 6, although they all get along, have definitely paired up with their favourites. Petunia and Duke are never far apart. Prince and Daisy are in love. Stan and Bud can usually be found side-by- side. But, in times of trouble, they are all together. They support each other, watch out for each other and, in their own way, love each other.

A quick little story about the depth of relationships with horses involves two of my rescues Bud and Daisy. Bud and Daisy are half-brother and sister paints that were rescued from a breed facility and separated. They were taken into rescue in the December and sent to different foster facilities. We adopted Bud in the February and then received a call in June/July asking if we would take Daisy. At this point they had been separated for about 8 months. We had Bud at a boarding facility with approximately 40 horses. Trailers with horses were always coming in and out and the horses, although curious, usually didn't react. The day we trailered Daisy in Bud was in a paddock at the side of the barn and couldn't really even see the trailer. The minute the trailer pulled onto the property Bud started going crazy and calling out. Daisy also started calling from the trailer. They obviously knew each other.

My husband immediately went and got Bud while I unloaded Daisy. It was like a scene out of a romantic movie. They ran towards each other, paying no attention to their surroundings, and immediately locked necks. No one can tell me those two didn't know each other and were so happy to be together.

Watching the episode on relationships in horses just reaffirmed what I already thought and confirmed that my plan when the time comes to euthanize Petunia is the right one. With the few people I have shared my plan with the reactions are mixed. Most disagree but after watching the movie, I don't care!

When the times comes to put Petunia down, we plan to do it on the farm in her favourite spot where she likes to lie in the sun and nap, where she is comfortable. The other horses will not be in the same paddock at the time however, but after we plan to open up the paddock and allow the herd to say their goodbyes and grieve in their own way before we bury Petunia on the property. They need to know that she is gone. They need to say good bye and pay their respects.

In the wild, when a horse passes on, the herd usually all walk by the horse and pay their respects. It also isn't unusual for the members of rival herds to also pass by, heads bowed, before returning to their own territory. Many herds also leave a guard horse behind to watch over the body for a day or so before moving on to catch up with the herd. I imagine that will be Duke as he has her back now!

Why should it be any different for my guys? Just because they live in a domesticated environment doesn't mean they are no longer horses. Or that they can no longer express their feelings in the ages old way of the horse.

The death of any family member, four-legged or two, is a very difficult time. Who are we to think that our animals don't grieve? That they won't miss their friend or that they need closure the same as we do.

"Listening to the Horse" has given me the confidence to believe in myself, to trust my own instincts when it comes to my horses and to realize that yes they are talking to me. I thoroughly recommend watching this movie. There are so many little things that you can learn to help you with your horses and, if you just begin to believe in yourself and in your horses that goes a long way to ensuring that your horses are happy and well looked after. No one knows, or no one should know, your horse better than you!

Krista Deering

How do you think the horse feels about that?

As a young child I grew up in a home with a violent father and a mentally abusive mother so at age 12 when I discovered the local stables run by a 73 year old man named Ted. I pestered him continually until he let me clean stables and yards and I believed I had found nirvana. Not only was I with horses but I had also found a sanctuary from the sadness and noise of home.

Ted was my mentor and in time helped me get my first pony, a palomino/Arabian cross buckskin gelding I named Monty. He was young and the first horse I started and he turned out to be a fabulous first pony.

At 20 years of age and still horse crazy, I bought my first small acreage and later purchased a beautiful Arabian stallion named Jerahmeel who had originally come to Western Australia from Sussex, UK.

His breeder and I became pen friends and corresponded regularly swapping stories of what we were doing with the horses. Jerahmeel stayed with me after the training business and stud I ran disbanded and my much loved friend, then a gelding, died in my arms after 23 years together at age 30.

I had a hiatus for a few years after losing him to deal with my grief, until one day in 2008 I saw an ad for an Arabian mare that wrenched at my heart. This little mare looked lost and frightened, so I journeyed to see her and made the decision to purchase her. I traced her history only to be horrified at the treatment she had received over some years, and so began the long healing journey for her. I wanted her to trust again and on that journey she made me a better person.

In our time together, I have seen the hurt in her eyes that I experienced as a child at home and this encouraged me to keep going with her and give her the chance of the peaceful life that I felt she deserved. Many people told me she was not "fixable" but they did not see what I did and that was the underlying sweetness and softness that I knew this mare had. She is now the beautiful, kind and trusting mare I always knew she could be.

The Listening to the Horse movie reinforced my beliefs that I was justified in allowing this mare (and others I have been fortunate enough to help) to speak out so she could learn to trust again.

Words from Mark Rashid on seeing the horses being broken as a boy and the older gentleman with him saying "How do you think the horse feels about that?" Such wise words and ones that I will carry with me every day to ensure I am always doing and will continue to do the best for my horses.

Karen Rohlf talking about not selling horses on if possible, and if we do have to, ensuring they get the best possible home. Horses are a long term relationship. My three are with me forever, God willing. Dr Robert Miller on starting horses later so they have time to develop, not only physically but also mentally. I have two 6 year old youngsters, one from the Arabian mare, who are just learning some of their starting lessons now.

Steve Halfpenny on the importance of groundwork which also relates to Dr Miller's statement. So much groundwork and walking can be done with younger horses so that by the time they are ridden they are relaxed, calm and trusting. My youngsters have been doing this since they were babies and they are relaxed and calm. If something does worry them, they know they are safe because they know I will never hurt them.

Mark Langley's calm and kind approach is a constant reminder of how we need to be with our horses. I love reading updates and watching his gentle approach.

Steve and Mark willingly share knowledge allowing those who listen to them to pass on information to others who need help.

They are not feeding their egos but genuinely want the best for horses and that is a lovely thing.

Everyone in the movie had ideas and ethos to pass on and there was so much wonderful sharing of information and that to me is the most important message of the movie – the sharing of knowledge.

We may not all be on the same page in relation to training methods, but we all want the best for all the horses out there.

Having spent the last 50 years of my life trying to help horses and learn as much as I can so I can do better, I loved the opportunity to listen to others, take in what they had to say and use that knowledge to improve what I do every day with my precious three.

Helping Baz to find his try

Let me introduce myself, here I am, a 56 year old woman with a lifelong equine obsession, childhood spent mucking around with ponies and most of my adult life working with horses on a professional basis, kind of specialising in rehabilitation of horses that had come unstuck and lost confidence in themselves, their job and often their people too. So you would think I would have all the answers, right? Wrong.

Meet Baz, at about 17hh (or maybe bit over) and the coolest, sweetest natured horse that ever strode the earth, a gentle giant, who loves all, people, other horses, dogs, cats, you name it, this guy is a friend to everyone.

We first met when he was a bit smaller, in a very muddy field in Brittany, he had been bred by a very good friend and was in a gang of weanlings hanging out in said field. Adeline was keen on breeding paint horses, but for some reason she put one of her mares to a Lusitano and Baz was the result. I wasn't even thinking of getting another horse, but this guy left his buddies and followed me around the field, ignoring the piles of hay being put out, in exchange for a cuddle and a scratch, he had huge knees and huge ears, soft friendly eyes and I fell in love.

One snag, I had no money to buy him, I thought about him most days, but that didn't fill the piggy bank. Eventually I decided to sell my horse to fund his purchase, that went well and when I phoned Adeline to tell her I had the money, she said he was sold! I was crushed.

What I didn't realise is that my husband had sold his beloved motorbike to buy Baz for my 50th birthday! How romantic is that? Hence, Baz had a long journey from Brittany to South West France, his new home and his new pals. And then he grew, and grew and grew some more for good measure! Backing him was the easiest thing in the world, hacking out all alone by the age of four, unfazed by pretty much everything, a total dude. All went well those first couple of years, he was a quick learner and wanted to please, had total trust in his people, I was taking things slow as he was such a big baby, and that is where we figuratively ground to a halt.

As I started asking more from him, particularly in the school. His Father had gone to the Olympics, so surely he must have some dressage talent? But Baz seemed more and more switched off by the whole thing; he would oblige, sort of, doing as little as he possibly could and I would use all my cunning skills to try and coax a bit more out of him, but it inevitably would result in frustration from me and misery for him.

He was typical of a lazy horse, but what bugged me is that I never really believed him to be lazy, he is bright of eye, he loves to play with anything he can get in his mouth or kick with his hoof, he wants to please, but something was stopping him being able to perform with any energy. To be honest, I was pretty stumped on how to motivate him, I have always found the hotheads easier than the cold bloods.

Baz has really good conformation, he turns heads wherever he goes, you would never suspect he had a physical problem, bring on my super osteo Kate. I was getting to my wits end with Baz, to my shame, I would sometimes get angry with him in the school, of course that didn't solve anything and left us both feeling pretty rubbish. So I got an equine osteopath to come and give him the once over, well the poor horse was so locked in his own body, these big muscles all in tension, that it explained how he just couldn't give me what I was asking of him, Kate, over several months unblocked the tensions, it was a bit like peeling an onion, as soon as one layer was got rid of another revealed. Baz loved his sessions and joined in with Kate at every opportunity, stretching, yawning, waving his willy.

Now for the start of Baz's remedial work, but sadly he was so imprinted with negative vibes from our unproductive schooling sessions that he actually did sigh as soon as we headed up to the arena, his head would go down and he would start gnawing his bit.

I have a lovely horseman friend Perry, who appeared in the Listening to the Horse movie. Lester Buckley recounted a story of a ranch horse who really didn't want to round up the cows, his trainer tried to hustle and bustle him, but the more the trainer did, the less the horse did, did that sound familiar or what? Thus the senior cowboy chucked the horse down to the junior cowboy to see what he could do, good luck!

Junior cowboy realised this horse wasn't lazy, he just lacked confidence and didn't want to get things wrong. How many people do you know who would rather not give something a go, than get it wrong? So why should a horse be any different? He decided to reward the tiniest "give" from the horse, which over the weeks dramatically changed the horse's point of view.

My new mission to reward Baz for every little give. I started inhand, each time he did something well I would stop asking, rub and praise him, and let him stand a while. Then, as he is such a playboy, I decided to teach him some tricks, lifting legs, stretching for carrots, kicking a ball, silly stuff like that, Baz loves it, now in the school we are doing liberty work and he is having FUN whilst building all those muscles up in the correct places to work in harmony with one another.

I may never have a dressage horse, but as long as I have a happy horse, who cares? I am lucky, he seems to hold no grudge and I am the wiser for it. One thing about horses, you NEVER stop learning.......

Rebecca Jameson Till

Could I have been the problem?

I'm thinking I should start this story by saying I am apparently a slow learner, so I hope I can 'speed up' the process for someone else. I know now my horse has been trying to tell me things for 10 years and I honestly thought I was listening.

And I was, but I was misinterpreting the messages so, unfortunately for my beautiful horse, I was constantly coming up with the wrong 'solution'. I must start at the beginning to clarify my journey.

After riding as a youngster with all the bravado that comes with youth, I had a hiatus from horses until I was 39, when I decided one day that I needed them back in my life.

I looked at the newspaper on a Wednesday and by Sunday I owned my first horse - a rising 8, unraced, chestnut Thoroughbred mare. She was both a dream come true and a nightmare. Physically, we went to hell and back many times with illnesses and injuries.

But both on the ground and under saddle, she looked after me like no other and I put all my trust in her to look after me. Don't get me wrong, she was feisty and could be scary but she could gallop, and man, did she love to gallop. And we did, everywhere. She never bolted and always slowed or stopped as soon as asked. I felt she was my soul mate.

I was bereft when I lost her after 18 years and never thought I would get another horse. Then my beautiful stock horse/thoroughbred cross gelding came along. He has everything in the looks department and being an eventer, I assumed he would be a brave and compliant animal.

The next few years were heartbreaking. The sad part of this tale is that I blamed every fault and problem on him.

He was the exact opposite to my mare. I know now that I channelled all my grief at her loss onto him. He never measured up in my eyes.

My ego of thinking I was a more than competent rider, meant that when he shied violently, or spooked at absolutely everything, or ran backwards at 100mph, it was him being a pig. I got to the stage I wanted to get rid of him, he scared me so much.

Don't get me wrong, he is a beautiful natured horse and there isn't a mean bone in his body. But under saddle he terrified me. I never felt in control.

I tried everything. Several different types of training, hundreds of dollars in supplements, you name it, I tried it. I had two different animal communicators converse with him, which was interesting, but nothing he told me led me to the conclusion, I was later to realise, is that I WAS THE PROBLEM.

No matter how hard I tried to relax and not anticipate something bad happening on every ride, it always did. In 8 years I had maybe 6 or 7 rides I could classify as enjoyable. If I stayed on him, it was a good ride. I am so sad for all the years I wasted making his life less than the happy, fun, pleasant life I wished for both of us.

Then I sat down one day and decided “Okay, I’m not getting any younger (I’m now 61). Something has to change. We have basically been doing the same thing for 9 years and it hasn’t got any better. WHAT AM I DOING WRONG?”

And therein lies the start of the new beginning - admitting that for all these years I have been projecting my fears onto this beautiful-natured horse and therefore not enabling him to feel safe and to have any trust in me.

How do I change things at the most basic level and undo so many years of behaviours that had become second nature?

I was already doing a version of Steve Halfpenny's 100 Miles a Month. I noticed a couple of years ago that spending at least 50% of my time on the ground instead of 100% in the saddle was making a BIG difference. But I still had those fears and apprehensions.

So I bit the bullet, withdrew some money from the bank, and ordered a custom made half breed saddle with a beautiful deep roughout seat and knee rolls. I had fallen out of my dressage saddle so many times I lost count. It just wasn't helping my confidence at all!!

Overnight, my attitude and confidence levels went through the roof! I no longer feel that heart pounding dread when he tenses at something, whether seen or unseen. I now have the confidence HE NEEDS to help him through it.

I am now able to see things from his perspective instead of just being a passenger, hanging on for dear life, feeding him negative energy, terrified that he is going to drop and spin as he was prone to do, leaving me in a heap on the ground.

Overnight, his behaviour changed also. He is a willing participant in our rides instead of a big spooky ball of fear. We have even had fast canters on a loose rein, with other horses no less, with no fear of a big shy coming out of the blue. We are having fun!! He still looks at things and asks questions, but

I answer them now and help him through instead of bullying him to 'comply'. But it was also a hard lesson to learn – to swallow my pride and admit I had been the problem all along.

I now speak to him, and of him, with affection and praise. I tell him every day how important he is to me, how much I enjoy his company, how much I love him, and how proud I am of him for forgiving me, in the blink of an eye, for taking almost 10 years to learn a lesson.

Had I made this realisation years ago, what a different tale I could tell. If I had Steve Halfpenny's insights a decade ago, I probably would have been able to change my mindset way back then without the need of an expensive saddle, but I am glad I have it, it is fabulous to ride in, ha ha.

So, my message to everyone following Steve, or whoever is helping you – open your hearts, open your minds, believe in yourself and above all else, believe in your horses. They are the truth. It was a long time coming, but what a gift my boy has given to me.

Wendy Bushell

Are you asking your horse to go away?

I am loving watching these movie episodes. After the second episode on groundwork. I walked to my pasture to just hang out with my mare. She is a very sweet horse that I have owned for 10 years and we get along great.

But after watching – I realized that for years I have mostly asked her to leave me from the ground and with my knowledge of ground work.

So I just wanted to see if she wanted to actually be with me. I walked in the pasture and she just watched me. I walked to her and patted her and told her why I was in the pasture. That I had just watched a movie about relationships with my horse.

She listen with ears up and a very pleasant face, I gave her a treat and a few good rubs. I then proceeded to walk around her paddock. She watched, turned and kept her eyes on me, but never approached me.

I could see her thinking, what is going on? Is she going to ask me to trot around freestyle? What is she going to ask of me? My mare was interested, but hesitate to approach or join in with my walk, but she did not want me to work her.

But after a bit of time, she just had to check me out, she started to follow me, about 6 feet behind me, but just walking, licking and chewing, like hum this is a bit weird! So I stopped, she stopped, but then approached. I gave her a treat with lots of warm rubs.

Then proceeded to my walk again, she followed close this time, next to me with ears up like where are we going. But soon bored with the walk she returned to the center of the grass paddock and watched me walk around.

After a bit more walking, I stopped and talked with the horse in the adjoining paddock, immediately she approached to see what was happening. I rewarded her with rubs, kind works and walked around her, she then connected up with me and we continued our walk around the paddock and ended at her stall.

It was a fun exercise for both of us, as she started to connect with me without a lot of movement of her feet as we have done in the past. She was happy, but the hesitation she showed me was not only surprising to me, it hurt a little as she is my heart horse and she are really bonded to each other, but I have built in a bit of a block, by sending her away from me at times and probably working her too much at other times, so she was a bit sceptical, we will continue to work on some down time together, not all work!

Going back to basics

For some people, being an equestrian is about riding as many different horses as possible and experiencing new opportunities. In my former years, I knew (or I thought I knew) riding different horses would make you a better rider so I followed that philosophy up until a certain point.

For me personally though, being an equestrian is about developing a bond and earning the trust of your horse. Getting to the point where when you think something, your horse does it, and just like that you two are one.

I've only gotten to this connection with two horses in my life so far and this movie series helped me deepen that connection with the horse I am currently with.

His name is Eagle and he's 15.2hh of pure Morgan craziness. I don't discriminate against breeds of any kind of animal, but Morgan was one of the last breeds I'd ever thought I would end up with. But there was something about him the first time I saw him and I've never regretted going with my gut instinct since.

All throughout my life I've heard countless horsemen and women talk about a horse that they knew was going to change their life the second they saw them. It had always baffled me that they could do that and I always wondered if it would ever happen to me. The more and more horses I had met, the more I began to wonder if it was really true. Was there some kind of trick? Are you born with it?

I think this moment finally hit me the first time I saw Eagle. He was out trotting around his field with his friends ready to come in for dinner and he looked way more like a wild Mustang to me than a Morgan.

It's fitting that I thought he looked like a Mustang because he has the personality to match; wild and free and not a care in the world. His mane was long, his trot was so expressive, and his face was filled with so much emotion. Something inside me ignited and kept nagging at me until fate came a knocking.

Not long after that, a friend had informed me that he was up for lease and even though I couldn't really afford it, I took the leap. Our first ride together was almost perfect, with a few speed bumps thrown in as we needed to get to know one another. But it was more than enough to seal the deal and confirm what I had believed the first time I saw him. Even my friend, who was taking videos of our first ride together can be heard saying in one of the videos, "Where is the paperwork? Sign it!"

Over the next year we spent time getting to know one another. I didn't really set any goals that first year beyond that as I didn't want to rush him. Plus we didn't have an indoor so he couldn't be worked most of the winter as much as he needed it. But boy, did he teach me a lot that first year. Along with his blazing personality and attention span the size of a teaspoon, came his never ending energy. It was a battle to try to get him in shape and keep him worked enough to stay happy. Come spring he was an absolute nut and I could barely keep up with him. There was a split second moment when I wondered if I was doing the right thing by leasing him.

The second year together brought some promise as I was able to keep him in shape that winter with a new indoor. This made for a much smoother transition that spring. He was much more level headed and by the end of the summer I was able to bring him to two dressage shows, where he once again turned into a nutcase. To give him credit, he was not entirely a nut but he just had become so distracted that we didn't have the connection we were starting to get and maintain at home. It was frustrating and I knew it was time to change things up a bit.

The start of our third year together is when this series came out and what brought inspiration to what I am doing with Eagle now. I had always been raised up in my equestrian career completely centered on riding. Riding lessons, riding clinics, riding shows, the list goes on. I wasn't naïve enough to not know there was more to horses than riding, but I had never been guided in that direction.

I had seen countless horsemen and women work with horses at liberty and tackless throughout my life. That to me was the ultimate goal of being an equestrian, to work with horses without any equipment and know that they trust you enough that they are willing to stay with you of their own free will. One horsemen in particular who I have followed for quite a few years now and who shows up several times on this series is Guy McLean. His performances are inspiring and what he can do with his horses is amazing, but beyond that this series really touched on how much he really does care for his horses. His heart and his passion for them are what make him so successful. Once you've won the heart of your horse, then there is nothing you two can't accomplish.

This movie series is what gave me the final nudge into going back to the basics with Eagle and not focus on riding so much.

My new goal became to try new things on the ground and do what makes him happy.

We have since tried liberty work, clicker training, and desensitizing with various "scary" objects and he is excelling beyond my wildest dreams. He overall looks the happiest and most relaxed I've ever seen. That in itself makes me happier than any blue ribbon ever could!

Michelle Berggren

Could it be due to pain?

I started riding at a very young age with no lessons. At 13 I bought a pony from the local dairy and ordered a pony cart from Sears catalogue. I put the harness on as directed and off we went. After a few accidents the pony figured it out with no help from me! As I got older I graduated to horses and rode bareback for years. When I was 28, I became a police officer.

A few years later I became a mounted patrol officer and finally had riding lessons. The lessons helped me a lot and then I felt I knew enough, so I quit taking lessons. I rode the streets and beaches of Miami, Florida and enjoyed the job immensely. I have been in several riding clubs through the years and enjoy trail and obstacle challenges. I retired in 2006 and had more time for riding and starting looking for another horse.

I started a civilian mounted unit and we began lessons again, now I am working on a video, Clip Clop Cops, Save our Mounted Police, The Last Mounted Soldiers. Which I hope to show communities how they can create civilian mounted units to help police departments and promote the horse as an effective police resource. We started having more lessons which helped me become a better rider, but no lessons taught what your videos taught. The communication portion of listening to the horse is what has always been missing in my life.

In 2008, my horses were getting older and it was time to look for a younger horse to keep up with me. A group of us drove to Jamestown, Tennessee and I came upon Hershey. He was tied up at a friend's barn, thin and no hooves. He was 18 months old and had been ridden up and down the Tennessee mountains with no shoes and now had no hooves left. The rescuer Bobby York, had a farrier come and put on Fiberglass hooves until his own would grow back. I took the horse home and gave him six months rest and regrowth and got his weight back up.

He threw his head constantly and fought the bit. After two years I was able to bring his head down, but still the head toss. Through the years I have changed bits, bridles and even tried bitless. I had dentists and vets check his teeth, mouth and no problems were noted. I attributed his head tossing to bad behavior from his previous life and tried to ignore it.

After watching your videos, I took him to a trainer, who advised me that his neck was out from the Atlas down to the shoulder. I then took Hershey to a chiropractor. After an hour and a half of adjusting and the horrible noises of vertebrae popping back into the right position, Hershey, after 10 years, is pain free. Hershey was instantly grateful to the chiropractor and you could see an instant change and doing the proper gaits a Tennessee walker should do.

I am ashamed he has been in pain for this amount of time and I did not know how to listen to him. I attributed his behavior to bad behavior and wrong bridles and bits. The trainer also told me my saddle was pinching his shoulders a bit, and I have changed my saddle as well. My seat is better and Hershey is now riding into my hands. I feel like I have a new horse, and a partner now. I look my horse in the eye now, I stay relaxed, and give positive commands and I listen to him as well. Thanks for a great series, which changed my attitude and my horse thanks you also!

Rebecca Card Swerdloff

Miniature horse adventures

I'm sure like everyone who has watched this series, I too have loved and been involved with horses my whole life. Although there was a time that I did take a break and didn't own any.

It wasn't until my daughter and her twin girls moved back to the island and purchased Miniature Horses my 'addiction' re-surfaced and I was back in it three-fold - Yes that is three minis. The first came when one of my granddaughter's asked me to help her purchase one, a yearling gelding named Jet.

After her first show season with him, she wanted to sell him, but I reminded her that she hadn't paid me back, so I kept him.

The second came two years later, when a friend's mare foaled - it was love at first sight! I was fine with the filly being at her house and I could visit, but when she said she was putting her up for sale.... Well... little LZ became horse number two!

You know what they say – Mini's are like potato chips – can't have just one, or in my case two.

I wasn't looking for another horse. I hadn't any even considered it, but when a member of our Miniature Horse Club posted a two-year-old blue roan for sale, that was it.

I went to look at him, he raced up to me and tried to bite me, and I gave him a tap on the nose, I knew he was the horse for me! Coda became number three.

Coda came to us as a stallion, and we had him gelded almost immediately. I had no idea LZ, my mare was such a floozy!

Coda fit in with the other two horses just fine, but for some reason I could not get the connection I was looking for. You see, Coda was an unexpected foal. The breeder had sold the mare, after having an ultrasound done, and being told she was not pregnant, they were wrong.

The people who purchased the mare were not experienced with foals, especially a colt, but thought they'd keep him. It wasn't long before he became unruly, biting, kicking and generally un-handleable. He was sent back to the breeder, and that's where I came in.

The biting and the kicking quickly resolved after he was gelded, but there was a distance. He didn't want to become part of the whole herd, the one that included me.

Jet and LZ are so oriented to people, so Coda's distance was hard to take. He did not want to be handled and learn things, so after a year, I decided to sell him hoping he would find 'his' person.

Several people were interested in him, but no buyers. I was okay with taking my time to sell him. The right person would come along and that was what was most important.

Then I watched Listening to the Horse... The title could not be more appropriate! It was the second show of the series, and as I watched and show ended, I was almost in tears. I went out to the stall where Coda was eating his night-time hay.

As usual when I entered his stall, he ignored me. I stood beside him and told him, we needed to talk. I apologized to him, saying that I really hadn't given him a fair shake. I had ignored him, hadn't spent any more time with him then I had to, and that I was wrong. I had given up on him and because I couldn't get a connection with him.

Coda stopped eating, raised his head and put his muzzle to my face, dropped his head down and then brought it back up to me. I rubbed his wither and told him things were going to be much different now. I would not sell him.

The next day, I went out after the morning feed and brushed everyone. I haltered Coda and I led him beside me without issue. No pulling, pushing, just an easy walk.

I thought I'd start easy and just ask him to do some side passes. Usually this was quite the ordeal, as he would push back every chance he got, and as usual, that's how it started. I looked at him and told him this wasn't working, and we needed to find another way. I pointed to my feet and then stepped to the side, he followed. I only had to tap his rear a tiny bit to get him to line up.

Okay, this was a fluke, right? So, we did it again, and again, and he followed every time in both directions. I knew he understood!

I didn't want to overdo it so after a few minutes I stopped and thought I try it with LZ. She did not understand what I was asking. That was okay, we have a different understanding, so I walked with her up and down the driveway.

Now, this was where I noticed a big change in Coda. He didn't want to be left out and barged in between LZ and myself. He wanted to walk with me, he wanted to learn, he wanted to connect! I cannot tell you how this has changed things. I have five dogs, and we communicate all the time. I did the same with the horses, but I don't think I ever waited for an answer. I never let them make a decision, not intentionally anyway. You've changed things for the better, in more ways than one. My horses thank you for giving me this very important AHA moment! Catherine.

Listening to Pete

After watching the documentary series Listening to the Horse, I decided that I needed to change the way I was interacting physical and emotionally with my horse.

As a little back story on my horse Pete. We have been together for 10 months. He went a long time not having his own person to love and care solely for him, we found each other and fell in love right away. Pete is part of my family. He wasn't just a horse we ride and put away after. He is what I needed and I was what he needed. We have always had a partnership and respect for each other. We both have a separation anxiety when we are not together. He loves to cuddle and be with me.

So Dec we moved stables for reasons that were better for both of us. And he seem to be adjusting well with new friends, his beautiful stall and pastures.

Two months ago he started bucking at a canter, with myself, my daughter and anyone who tried to ride him. For the life of us we couldn't figure out why. His tack never changed, his personality was the same on ground and in walk trot. I decided let's start from the beginning and work our way back to riding. I was going to start with our liberty.

We have always done liberty from day one but that was drastically changing for him as in misbehaving. Running towards visitors who were watching, not listening to my cues and not wanting to be with me. He was just all over the place and the connection was a bit misplaced and out of reach.

We have always been close but the training and liberty were our issues little did I know they were going to be corrected by correcting one important element.

I started watching Listening to the Horse and had that moment of realization I need to listen to him and find out what he wants. So the next day I went to see my horse and as I was grooming him and getting him ready for Liberty I was talking to my horse Pete and told him he would be choosing his activity today.

I wasn't going to put pressure on him or have an agenda, we were just going to do what he wanted. I led him into the arena, and took off his lead rope and placed my hands on his face and looked deep into his eyes. I said to him "You are choosing what you want to do today, you choose your activity and I will follow your cues." My horse then decided he was going to head to the middle of the arena and roll.

But then something magical happened. He came back to me as I was watching him from a distance. I gave him a rub on his forehead and a big smile. He went back to the end of the arena and looked around gave a few excited bucks and trots but he came back to me each time. As he chose his own agenda he always came back to where I was. It is almost as if he was saying I want to play with you and be with you. That connection we misplaced was found.

The next day I did the same but had a friend watch in the arena with us. It was a test to see if he would still want to be with me or misbehave again with an audience. I took him to the middle of the arena and we stood together for a few minutes and I told my horse we can play together if he wanted. I walked on and he followed right beside me, we turned and zigzagged and halted and trotted together and just had our time of fun. Not once did he leave my side, he was focused on me and nothing else. I believe that if I didn't stop and listen we would be still disconnected and not realizing why.

So with this corrected I decided let's tack him up and go for a ride in the arena the next day. I walked and trotted on him and did a few things on him but I couldn't canter. It was my fear on top of my fear of cantering. I wasn't sure if he would buck. I had a friend jump on him and try it out he bucked. I just couldn't figure it out. Why was he bucking?

The next day I decided my daughter and I would take him out. I rode him around for a bit nothing special just walk trot and I gave him very loose reins to see what he wanted. He would pick his trot up to a quick one. I put my daughter on him and she did the same but this time, she asked for a canter he bucked a couple of times and finally after five minutes of trying my horse gave in.

He went from a trot to a canter beautifully. The praise and excitement could be heard everywhere. We gave him head rubs and kisses and oh the tears. I mounted him this time and said ok I'm going to try myself. We walked, trotted and went into a beautiful canter. I truly believe that I was missing my horse's cues and not listening to what he needed. When we started communicating with each other and really listening our partnership and closeness was found again.

By starting with our relationship at liberty and listening to him has corrected our riding. My one important piece of advice to others would be. Listen and let your horse chose what he wants sometimes. We ask so much from them and they give us what we want every time, sometimes we need to stop and let them ask us for things. That's what a partnership is.

Tanya Rivard

The power of the bladder meridian technique

Thank you so much for sharing your work and sharing this series with the public! Listening to the Horse was perfect for touching on so many aspects of owning, training, riding, and caring for horses. I found every episode beneficial, and learned something new to think about, or validate what I already thought I knew. I found great joy in that feeling of validation through many of the comments and suggestions made by your featured professionals.

Truly, I had several 'a-ha' moments throughout the series, but the most significant takeaway for me was the Bladder Meridian technique! We have had chiropractic and acupuncture done on all three of our horses at one time or another to address various things, and witnessed the 'release' when it comes.

What I didn't know is how remarkable this technique is, the science behind it, and the amazing results by doing it! Immediately after seeing the demo done in the series, I went out and researched more. The next day I went out and performed the technique on all three horses and WOW, just WOW!

I started with our 29 year old QH gelding who is semi-retired (former working ranch horse, and pleasure horse for last 14 years), has moderate arthritis, and recently diagnosed with Navicular. Doing the Bladder Meridian technique, I immediately experienced the eye fluttering and some fidgeting. As I hovered over the areas he was telling me were tense, he had significant releases in the neck, lower back, hips and hock areas! It was simply heart-warming to watch him blow, lick, chew and turn to look at me. Thanks Mom!

Our 16 year QH gelding (a former competitive reiner) whom we now use for trail and pleasure, showed me huge releases with 6 long yawns while I worked on his hind end, and he blew loudly with licks and chews with tension released in his neck. I was amazed by his reactions, and on him, I found that I could actually feel heat radiating from the energy/tension releasing while my hand hovered over the areas he was reacting to.

Needless to say, by the time I was done (about 45 minutes) he was uber relaxed, head hung low and I know he was thankful.

Different story for our newest 12 year old QH, another trail horse. In the year we've owned him, his temperament is more 'worried' and he doesn't seem to relax readily. When I started above his eyes, and moved to his neck I could tell he was having some reaction/release immediately, but he was very fidgety, head tossing, and moved around quite a bit. I do believe he was releasing some tension (apparently a lot), yet I was barely able to continue through his neck, back and haunches as he was just dancing around too much.

Typically he does not behave that way when I groom or touch him. This makes me believe he's got LOTs of tension, and my job will be to slowly show him that the 'release' will feel good, and he too will love it when he can tolerate it. I will take a slower approach with him.

The takeaway from learning about the Bladder Meridian technique is it's a fabulous way to release tension before or after a ride, and especially for wellness/longevity in the normal care of our horses. All three horses were very demonstrative with their expressed "releases" making me realize that we do not know how much tension our horses are carrying around with them from day to day.

Feeling the heat on my hand as I hovered over the 'focus areas' was telling me the tension was releasing. Fascinating!

The trick for me was being patient in a particular area and wait for the release...some bigger than others, but the release does come! I believe over time there could be no expression of tension, however, if a certain area persists, I would assume there could be subluxation and do a chiropractic visit.

The true test of tension release was the head turns for treats afterwards, and all three showed improvement, especially my 29 year old! He continued yawning after I turned him out making me think he really enjoyed our session!

This technique surely has wonderful benefits, and I'm hoping to see the results under saddle to see if they are more supple. Just experiencing this over time I believe our horses will stand quietly and know the goodness that is coming!

The phenomenon of the Bladder Meridian technique gave me a great sense of joy, and adding another fine way to build trust. We will bond more with our horses when we regularly implement this form of care and this technique will now be a part of our regular maintenance. Can't wait to try this on a couple of my friends' horses. They will be thrilled. I may even go for a certification... It's that good! Keep the good work coming!

Terri Carvey

One step at a time

I had an amazing aha moment from the Listening to the Horse film. I purchased a Missouri Fox Trotter mare last summer who had "some baggage". She had several owners throughout her life but one person stood out for her, an older gentleman who rode her with patience and love. Unfortunately, he became sick and had to be put into a nursing home. She never seemed to get over him and being passed from person to person didn't help.

I am a forever home so thought maybe I could give her that connection again with time. Little did I know what I was up against until I tried to ride her once she was home.

I saddled her and got on her no problem but then she turned toward the gate and bulked all the way back to it. I tried to turn her but she just hung her head in confusion and sadness. I dismounted at that time because something was very wrong. Working with her on the ground didn't seem to help so I let her sit for six months and just be a horse giving her a chance to decompress from whatever had hurt her.

I loved on her daily but only gave the amount of attention and affection that she could handle. Some days she was loving other days she was grumpy. Also during this time I got to work, doing background on her.

Apparently, she had been pushed and pushed by her last owner to the point that nothing was good enough. Not only pushed but put into unsafe situations that terrified my mare into meltdowns. There were even rumors that the horse and rider got into a dangerous accident leaving both scarred.

To tell you the truth I had no idea where to start helping her with this frightening news. When the video talked about the fact that a horse's "try" needs to be fostered, it clicked that this just might be the help she needed. Someone had broken her try and she had given up hanging her head in a sad state of hopelessness.

The story of the cowhorse who was encouraged with every little step until he was excited about working again set off an idea in our family-run barn. My mom put in a thought, maybe we should start small and encourage her on the ground since she just doesn't want to be worked at all? So I started her in the aisle with halter and lead line.

I took a few steps forward making sure not to pull on the lead. She took a step forward and I praised her. She looked at me like, "really?" Then we did this over and over. It got to be a game in her mind; she was so excited to be doing good! She then started testing me: "What if I put my front foot forward? What if I put my back foot forward? What if I move my body slightly forward?" All my responses were an enthusiastic "Great job!" She just couldn't get enough of the praises for the try! I even got some nuzzles in the middle of it.

One time she just wanted to stand and process the experience. Another time she wanted to walk several steps. I eventually walked her to her stall but she wasn't ready to quit so we did it all again. I'm blown away that she needed the praises at the very start of the time with her not just when we were in the arena. I now know what I can do along with groundwork to start reprogramming all her bad memories into positive time with a person.

We have to get back to the way she was loved by the older gentleman where she flourished. It's in there; she is so smart. Missouri Fox Trotters are known for their trying to please attitude and love of people, but that personality can be gravely hurt when harsh training comes their way. It makes me more determined to fight for her and do right by her.

I am hoping to one day expand this process under saddle so I can ride her again... small steps lots of praise all the way. Not only did we get closer to that goal but it was a wonderful bonding time for us and fun for me. Thank you, the whole series was very validating on many things I am doing right, and the rest was just great learning! Karen Schuster.

My name is Lucy

My name is Lucy and I'm 14 years old. I recently acquired my first horse the love of my life, an Appaloosa names jack. Jack was 5, green unbroken not gelded and I was a green rider! Perfect combination for a disaster lol but Jack was my love my first horse and I was determined to prove everyone wrong and train my gorgeous boy.

We got off to a wonderful start with some basic groundwork, he even let me ride him bareback. I was so excited. This beautiful boy had the most gorgeous personality. We enlisted the help of a trainer and then your series became available. I was so excited to watch it and gain further knowledge to develop my relationship with this boy.

Sadly just a few days before your documentary began my boy developed a very serious case of colic and died. My heart was broken, however my mum and I sat down through tears and watched your series. I had started lessons on another horse Teddy, but my heart just wasn't in it. No matter how hard I tried I felt I was betraying my Jack by loving another.

Through watching your series I realised that horses pick up on our emotion and understand. I was letting Teddy know the pain I felt, the guilt I felt and my heart was closed.

After watching series 3, I had a lesson on Teddy. I quietly whispered to him that I loved him but my heart was broken. I couldn't find the energy to trot that day only walk around the arena.

My beautiful Teddy looked after me and we just walked around and around. I shed a lot of tears as we walked. I attempted a trot and fell off, Teddy came straight back to me and stood over me with so much concern.

I thanked him for helping me, he even paused at Jack's burial site as if in respect. With each series I became stronger in the knowledge that Jack had brought Teddy to me. My instructor could not believe how much Teddy looked after me, he would just lay his head on my shoulder while I sobbed.

Each series gave me ideas to try out, things to do with Teddy, how to fit his saddle, how to pick up on colic, how to recognise his trot change and my riding position.

The most powerful lesson I learned was to listen to this beautiful boy who was trying to connect with my heart. I have made the decision to buy Teddy and together we will move mountains with Jack's spirit riding along with us both. All the people involved were amazing we have added them onto my mum's Facebook so we will always be connected. I cannot wait to start my journey with Teddy and I want to truly thank you for bringing this into my life exactly when I needed it.

Jo and Lucy Clark

Are they lonely?

This seven-part docu-series is the most insightful, fascinating and informative series I have ever watched. This movie delves into all aspects of the horse and rider, from horsemanship & training to care & feeding. It was fascinating to learn how horses think and process their thoughts. How they learn from your release of pressure is their reward.

It was very interesting how now days people are starting colts to early as young as eighteen months causing kissing spine, when in the past a colt was not started till four or five years of age. I learned that a horse's spine does not close tell they are six or seven.

The movie really made me think about how forming a relationship with my horse is so very important. How a horse understands much more than we humans give them credit for. How when we ask them to do something they actually process and try to figure out for themselves what we are asking.

I am a dressage rider and found the episode on riding to be extremely informative, how the trainers defined how a horse truly works in collection and getting a horse in collection is not done in the front of the horse but from his hind quarters. How a horse has to be fit and have strong muscles especially in the hind quarters to be able to go into collection.

In turn riding a horse in collection keeps the horse fit enabling the horse to live a longer healthier life. My favorite was when one trainer said, "collection is a private conversation between horse and rider". The information on riding with less is more, is great. The less pressure from bits and nosebands can only make the horse feel freer and more comfortable.

I was excited to get to the barn and experiment with this new-found knowledge. I always talk to my horse while grooming him he just loves when I curry his neck, he puts his head way up in the air and just loves it.

After grooming and tacking him up we walked around the arena or warm up, I talked with him, I looked into his eyes and asked him how he felt, I could feel him tell me he felt stiff, I will never forget that the feeling of communication, it brought tears to my eyes. When riding I thought more about what I wanted him to do instead of using a lot of aids. It was great he was light to my aids and we worked together as one, it was the best rides we have every had together.

I board my horse so I am not in charge of his feeding the parts of the movie on feeding and how horses eat was really worth watching. I am in control of his care and all the information on care of their hooves and daily maintenance was very informative.

I really enjoyed watching how the teeth are floated I have never seen dentistry done and was amazed on how many teeth they have. Watching the horses forage in the wild in a herd made me think and wonder if maybe my horse was lonely. He has his own paddock where he can see all his friends, but they are not all together in a herd...are they lonely?

I would like to thank everyone who took part in the making of this docu-series. I enjoyed every episode and could watch it again and again. I am hoping horse lovers all over the world enjoyed it as much as I.

Linda Morton

Considering your horse's health

Listening to the Horse for me was a great review of some information I already knew along with new information for me to ponder and implement into my relationships with my horses. The film was a great reminder of the importance of remaining teachable and being open to new knowledge and ideas. It is far too easy to get set in our own ways of doing things but we have so much we can learn from each other as we all strive to do what is best for our horses.

Probably the discussion that had the greatest impact on me in the film was the section on collection and how it affects the health of our horses.

I primarily trail ride with my horses and although I have done some lessons and worked on collection in an arena riding environment, I have never considered the importance of what this actually does for my horse.

It was mentioned in the film that collection exercises help develop the muscles a horse needs to better carry a rider and keep their body healthy. This is the first time I have made this connection that it is important for me to spend the time to do some collection exercises with my horses and this will actually help on the trail as well as keep my horses strong for many years to come. I also liked the discussions about what true collection really is Vs false collection. I will be planning to implement some collection exercises into my riding routine. This will be a great thing for me to do around home when I'm not able to make it out to the trails.

Along the same line, the other point that had an impact on me from the film was the discussion about not starting horses too early.

I currently have a Rocky Mountain gelding that will be turning two this summer. It has been a lifelong dream for me to raise and train a horse from an early age and build a relationship that lasts the entire lifetime of that horse. My Rocky joined my family when he was weaned and I am looking forward to fulfilling my dream with this horse. His happiness, health, and learning are all very important to me.

Where I live in Montana, there is a lot of pressure to get horses under saddle for their first rides as two year olds and really to have them ready to work long hours in the saddle by the time they are four.

This film had the best explanation I have heard on why it is important to wait for the horse to mature physically and not to rush training the horse under saddle. I will be training this youngster primarily on my own. I have already felt the peer pressure to get a saddle on him and start getting some rides in on him. I really liked that your movie stressed the importance of delaying the physical stresses that come from riding too early.

I also liked that it was clear from your film that much can be accomplished on the ground. It made me feel that I will be making a really good decision for my horse and his future health to delay riding him to early and to focus on ground work at least for another year or more and then to keep his rides very short when I do start to ride.

Thank you for helping me not feel guilty or like I am behind the game by waiting to start my young horse under saddle. The section on the hackamore was also very helpful as I make plans for my young horse. I had already planned to start in a hackamore but the explanation about proper fit for the function of the hackamore was very useful.

Finally, I enjoyed the sections about learning to listen to my horses and trying to figure out what they are communicating to me. I found the interview with the animal communicator to be especially fascinating. It opened my eyes to a new level of communication with my horses that I never knew was possible. I am going to try to listen more and develop that skill of actually hearing what my horse is saying to me.

Rachel

Have faith in yourself

We just finished watching “Listening to the Horse” and, not only did I learn a lot that I can use in my journey going forward, it also served to reaffirm that what I am doing with my horses is the right thing to do.

My journey began 5 years ago this May 2019. I was 53 years old and, although I had always loved horses, I had never ridden. In fact, I was fine on the ground with the horses and on their backs at a walk, but the minute they started to trot...I wanted off.

Learning to ride had always been a “bucket list” item and my wonderful husband decided to buy me a series of six riding lessons the Christmas of 2012.

It took me until May 2013 before I actually got up the courage to go for that first lesson and discovered that the anticipation of the lesson was way scarier that the actual lesson. (Believe in yourself and picture the best not the worst.)

By July I was four lessons in when I was thrown off the horse I was riding. He spooked at the mounting block, reared up and with my inexperience it just went from bad to worse. I ended up with a few cracked ribs and I suspect a broken bone in my foot as I still can't wear high heels. I swore I was never riding again!!

A gentleman at the barn picked me up, dusted me off and let me cry for 10 minutes then basically forced me to get back up but on his horse, on the lead line. I was petrified but, I did it. I took the next day off then showed up for a lesson the following day which is when I was introduced to Petunia the horse I would be riding from now on.

That moment, when I met Petunia, everything changed. Being new to riding I didn't know anything about "chestnut mares", or being over horsed or the difference between a quiet school horse and Petunia (sometimes ignorance is bliss). I just knew she was the one. She had attitude, was and still is feisty, she is definitely not an affectionate horse but we connected and she has taught me so much about riding and horsemanship. She is a communicator, if she doesn't like something she lets you know it. Sometimes that is just a glare, a twitch of her ear or a toss of her head, but other times it can be a full on head down, backside in the air buck. But I learned to understand her, her signals, her moods and we became a team.

By November I didn't want anyone else riding her and neither did she. So again, being inexperienced and not knowing any better, my husband bought her for me that Christmas after only riding for 6 months. And boy, what an adventure we have been on since then.

After purchasing Petunia I discovered that my husband of 20 odd years also loved horses...go figure. So, you guessed it, we bought another horse. In the year I had been at the boarding/lesson barn with Petunia we had watched Duke be sold and returned a couple of times.

Every time he was brought back he would be put back out to pasture and left for indefinite amounts of time without much, if any, human contact. Then the young girls would bring him in, and without any sort of warm up, put him through a jump course and then wonder why he would be sore/lame the next day.

Duke is a fairly large, stocky quarter horse with a lot of attitude. He is very stoic and would just do what he was asked, almost a learned helplessness, as he knew there was no relief for him. He was usually returned because of attitude and because he was sold as a trail horse but the purchasers tried to jump him. Finally, the last straw came for my husband when he saw a guy get on Duke at the barn and ride him way too aggressively, in our opinion. So out came the cheque book.

Duke is now 17 years old and has been with us 4 years this summer. He still has attitude but he is much happier here. He doesn't get ridden a lot but does like to get out on the trails.

At this point in my story we were still living just outside of Toronto, Canada and boarding Petunia and Duke. Which is great and doable with just two horses. Except.... In June 2015 a skinny, unkempt, 18 month old rescue colt showed up at the barn. It was love at first sight.

Again my lack of experience and knowledge came into the picture. I was told Prince, as I ended up naming him, was a gypsy vanner pony and would top out at about 14.2 and would be a great size horse for me. I am on the shorter side. Don't know what I was thinking....but we bought him. I had no idea how to train a young, never been handled, young stud...lol. Luckily, he has the most amazing patient personality and we have learned together. The old saying "green horse, green rider equals black and blue", was not the case for us and I truly believe that is because we have gone so slowly together. He is now 5 and we are just really starting to train him now. Yes he has been backed and ridden, by me only, but we have only done very basic work at a walk and trot. By the way, turns out he is a paint/shire cross who was destined for the meat market. At 5 he now stands 15.3, is 1100 pounds and hasn't finished growing.

So you would think that with three horses we would be done. But no, along came Bud and Daisy. A half brother and sister who had been rescued by the SPCA. Both had been locked in stalls for the first 3 and half years of their lives. Bud was only brought, as a stud, to service the mares. Poor Daisy I don't think was ever let out and she was badly injured when she was rescued. It took both of them a long time before they would freely go in and out of their stalls.

We adopted Bud first at the age of 4 and he was terrified of everything. We couldn't put him out with the herd (there were about 20 horses living out) because he was never socialized as a youngster. He would just tear blindly around the pasture seating and shaking until we went to get him. I was warned repeatedly that he was "wild", "dangerous" and would never be ridden. But he now lives in a herd of 6, he is comfortable with new horses coming in and out and has been ridden by beginners and children.

About 5 months after adopting Bud, I received another call from the SPCA saying that they had his sister Daisy and that they couldn't adopt her out because of her attitude. They asked if we would take her, no adoption fees, just give her a home. Of course, I said yes. Daisy is the same age as Bud and we have had them both for almost 3 years now. Daisy needed a lot of time to learn to trust and gain her confidence. We didn't ask anything of her until she told us she was ready.

She is now the most affectionate horse in the herd and I use her for lessons with kids as young as 5. She is extremely gentle and trusting, still a little head shy with sudden movements and hates a bit, but her injuries where on her nose and face so understandable. It was after adopting Daisy that we realized with 5 horses we needed our own property.

So not one to do things in half measures, we bought a 28 acre property in Nova Scotia, Canada. Almost 2000 kilometers away from our home in Ontario. The property had two houses and lots of land but that was it. We have been here 3 years this October and have built 5 paddocks, fenced a pasture, built a six stall barn, a hay barn, a round pen, and outdoor arena and an indoor arena. Yes we have been busy and have had to learn everything as we went.

Since then we also have a sixth horse on the property. Stan is a 15 year old great-great-grandson of Secretariat. His owner is in the Canadian Navy and is currently deployed so we are looking after him while she looks after our country. When Stan first came to us he was incredibly skinny, unfortunately thoroughbreds are hard keepers but I am happy to say he is gaining weight, playing with the herd and has made himself right at home.

So in 5 years I have gone from not even being able to ride to owing 5 horses (plus Stan), owning and operating a 28 acre facility, taking in horses that need temporary board and actually being asked my opinion on how I would do things with the horses.

A lot of what I have done with the horses has been instinctual, it just felt like it was the right thing to do.

Watching the movie validated what I have done and gave me some brilliant ideas of what to do with them going forward. I like to think that I do listen to what they are telling me and that, as a result of that I have 6 happy, healthy horses.

The first thing people say when they come to visit, after are you crazy, is that your horses all look so happy and to me, that is the ultimate compliment. My horses are social, they are easy to catch, they aren't afraid of people and they look forward to riding.

What I have learned from the movie is to continue to listen to the horses, to picture the best outcome (not the worst) and they will see that image and try to do it for you, if I walk into a situation that is uncomfortable for me… it is probably uncomfortable for my horses as well.

Horses are very forgiving and don't mind me making mistakes if my heart is in the right place and I put their best interests first. I am here on the farm alone quite a bit as my husband travels for work so it is important that I keep myself healthy, both physically and mentally, so that I can be there for them.

Going forward I plan to host a "horse night" for some of the riders in my area so we can watch the episodes, with wine, and discuss what we have learned and how we can improve the life of our horses going forward.

In my neck of the woods, a lot of the horse farms are run by women, sometimes with husband help and sometimes not. I think it is important to band together and create an environment where we can help each other when needed, discuss our horses and how to care for them and share experiences with each other.

At the end of the day I think this movie should be a mandatory watch at all boarding/lesson facilities. Even for those people who do not actually own a horse as there is so much information in the seven episodes that I wish I had known before I began my journey.

Krista Deering

Every horse matters

I have been taking lessons at multiple barns for a little over a year & half. I'm an older women & have discovered my new found passion - horses! I've always have been an animal lover but there's just something majestic about the horse.

The Listening to the Horse series really spoke to me on so many levels. I ride many lesson horses & love them all. Some more than others. It's hard not to bond with them. I couldn't progress as a rider without them however, sometimes I do feel empathy for them. They have us pulling, bumping, & teetering on their backs. The lesson horses I ride are geriatric in age. I've always tried my best to be soft in my hands & light in my seat but I'm still learning.

I feel for them. After watching the Listening to the Horse episodes I went to one of the barns & I was told I couldn't ride my favorite horse because we were getting "too accustomed" to each other. Needless to say I was disappointed. I was told to ride a pony that is very grumpy & bites when you groom him & tack him up. Some of the lesson students call him the donkey aka ass because his countenance is gray. He looks like a donkey & acts like an ass according to most riders at the barn. He's a blue roan. I've ridden him before but not for quite some time.

He is grumpy about grooming. He's sensitive & doesn't like a lot of pressure from the brushstrokes. As soon as I got out the brushes out he threw up his head & hit me in the nose. It was an accident but I then had a bloody nose. I stuffed my nose with Kleenex & started grooming him. He was trying to bite me more than usual, any chance he could get. I was thinking "Wow, his biting problem has gotten a lot worse!" Then, I was grooming his back leg & he almost pooped on my head.

Tacking up it was the same story he kept trying to bite me. I lead him to the ring & he tried to bite me again. That never happened before. My ride seemed off & my instructor commented on my lack of confidence.

I mentioned the horse's biting problem.

His comment was to hit the horse because that behavior was not allowed. In my mind I was thinking something is wrong w/the horse maybe that is making him grumpy and hitting isn't my style. There had to be another solution. After the lesson I figured I'd probably be riding him again the next week since I was told I needed a break from my heart horse.

I did some thinking & planning. I just recently became a reiki practitioner. So I placed a rose quartz stone in my half chaps. I sent pink loving light to the horse on my drive to the barn. I had my pocket full of bite size horse treats for positive reinforcement. I had frankincense essential oil in my bag.

When I arrived at the barn I was told I could ride either grumpy pants or my usual ride. I already had my game plan down so I decided to start grooming donkey man.

I let him smell the frankincense & he seemed curious. I rubbed some on him. I started to groom him. Every time he turned his head to attempt to bite me I wiggles my elbow like a chicken wing. When he looked forward I gave him a treat. I did this multiple times.

He stopped his attempts to bite & even let me tighten the girth with no problems. His eyes softened & we seemed to connect.

I felt like he was misunderstood. He just wanted to be treated like he mattered not just a ride. I want to thank you for the series. I've learned so much & am so glad there are other horse people who value horses for their heart & souls! Sometime in the future I'll have a forever horse to call my own :)

Mi.

Stabling and health

I'm born and raised in Germany, starting riding at age 7. Had my first own large pony at age 11. Upgraded to a 16h2 Hanoverian when I was 14 and due to behaviour issues that caused me frequent ER visits and x-rays, sold him a year later.

I moved to Canada when I was 19 and after I finished college and got a car, I picked up riding again when I was 24. For two years now, I have my own smaller 15h2 horse again.

In Germany 90% of people had their horse in a budget friendly 24/7 stall with straw bedding. Brick walls, no window, no chance of social contact. Solitary confinement like a criminal in a 14x14ft box.

Out of the 150 stalls between 3 different buildings, 20% had a window to the outside which were opened on nice days for 12hrs.

For a horse owner it was almost impossible to take care of your horse by yourself for 7 days a week. So we part boarded out our horses to beginner riders or single moms who didn't have the time or money to fully own a horse. On average a part boarder paid $150 a month for 3 rides per week. Lessons were very cheap, $12 for 60min group lessons. A private lesson was $50 with a high level off site coach.

In summer we'd pay an extra $100 per month to get a grass pasture assigned with up to 6 other horses and their owners.

It took some coordinating to get your horse 2hrs of grass time and you had to be there to bring it out and turn back in. Or pay additional $50 a month for the barn staff to turn out your horse for 3hrs each morning. Our horses would spend no more than 2min running across the pasture, sniffing each other and immediately focusing on grazing before time was up and they were put back in their stall.

Outdoor board was available and a bit cheaper but also didn't include full use of the facilities (no use of arenas, tack locker or hot walker). Around my area with 5 big cities, each about 1 million population each, western riding or groundwork/horsemanship was for tree huggers and frowned upon by English riders. Even here in eastern Canada, most English riders lack the ability to listen to their horse and rather bark orders all day long.

Coming to Canada, I soon realised, most horses live outside even in the frigid -25 Celsius winter months. In summer we also get a month of up to +45 Celsius due to high humidity.

Having the horse put in a stall every day increases the monthly board on average by 35%. Most barns don't have a large enough barn to offer a stall to each horse that is boarded on property (30 horses, 12 stalls). One other major difference I found between the countries is that mucking out in Canada is always done by the barn owner to ensure it gets done daily and minimal amount of usable wood shavings get thrown out.

I do however see quite frequently that show horses here only get individual turnout for 8 to 12 hrs a day depending on the weather. Again, no social contact allowed to avoid injuries and marks on their skin.

The biggest difference I learned was, horses in Canada live to 25yrs on average and get ridden into their early 20s. In Germany I only ever met 1 horse that lived to 31 out of the 200 horses on property at the show jumping barn I was with for 8 years.

Many German horses had to be retired around age 15 due to lameness. Many died of colic, the vet was out every week just for another colic case. Pouring a bucket of liquid into the horse with a funnel and hose going through the nose into the stomach. It was normal to feed a horse 4lbs of high energy, fat and fibre pellets and 1lb of oats per day, spread out over 3 meals and 2 times a day a load of hay. Some horses would continue to eat their straw bedding.

Cribbing, weaving, head bobbing, etc. At least one mental condition visible every second or third stall when walking through the aisles.

I wished my mother back then would have stood out in a good way to me and put my horse on outdoor board, even if it meant I would have had to walk 15 minutes each way in wind and weather every day just to fetch my horse off the big field where it would have lived in a herd of 20.

I'm grateful for having experienced both scenarios first hand and being able to allow my first own horse to have grown up on a large field with a herd and now living a comfortable life with horse friends. The horses here are so much more independent from us humans. They feel like they don't need us in order to survive where a horse in Germany would beg for your attention whenever a human walked past them. Like dogs in a shelter, waiting to be adopted.

Aylin Schiefer

A 15 Year Old Experiments

In the documentary 'Listening To The Horse' Lester Buckley talks about a method called 'Try and Release'. 'Try and Release' is a method of training for all horses, particularly for young or wild horses, that breaks down steps, encourages and helps the horse to understand what you are asking them to do.

When you are first teaching your horse this method, you should start with something simple: for example, the 'Back Up'. Initially when you start, you only want him/her to either drop their head or shift their weight back; this is called the 'Try'. When they do this, you should instantly let go of all pressure and give them a rub; this is called the 'Release'. This helps the horse to understand what you are asking for and helps the horse to not get confused.

Lester Buckley's method of 'Try and Release' really worked for his horse and I am interested to try it with my horse. In the 'Listening To The Horse' documentary, Lester Buckley talks about his well-bred cow-pony that had no interest in working cows. He decided to use the 'Try and Release' method to help his horse engage with him and the cow.

Every time he rides his horse in a pen with a cow, and the horse shows any sign of trying to have energy, he would hop off and put his horse away. He only worked for ten minutes a day, but once he started rewarding the horse for the slightest try, within three weeks his horse was moving the cows, and he was bright and full of energy. If you reward the horse for trying, they enjoy it. If you are critical with them, however, we can shut them down.

Lester Buckley used this method, and over time he proves that this method of ‘Try and Release’ helps horses like his cow-pony to enjoy work and learn faster.

I used this method with my horse Bella for teaching the Roll Back. At first, her turns were quite dull and slow; she was also getting confused and not understanding what I was trying to ask her. Then I started to use the ’Try and Release’ method. I pointed her on a straight at a trot. After a couple of strides, I asked her to stop. As soon as she did, I released all pressure, said “good girl”, and gave her a rub. Then I did it again. This time when she stopped, I said “good girl” but I asked a little more: I asked for a weight shift to the left. Once she had done that, I released all pressure, said “good girl” and gave her a rub. The next time I asked for one step, then released and finished the session. The next day, when I asked her to stop and take one step to the left, she did it right away so I released, and gave her a rub.

Then I tried it again, but this time when I asked for the one step instead she gave me two. As soon as she did, I gave her a rub and finished the session. The next day, I asked for a little more and, within a week, her turns were sharp and full of life. Now Bella really enjoys sporting.

I found Lester Buckley's method of training to be really helpful and my horse responded really well. I would definitely recommend using this method and I will be using it in the future.

Angela Pengilly.

Horses understand more than you realise

Listening to the Horse Movie was a wonderful heartwarming enlightening experience. I have always thought there was more to my horses then I was lead to believe. Every presenting horse person on Listen to the Horse had some new knowledge that was an Aha! moment and I thank you so much for putting this film together.

I wish for everyone who has anything to do with a horse to watch Listening to the Horse to make this a better world for the horse. There are too many experts in the horse world that know everything. One of my Aha! moments from watching Listen to the Horse was with the rider position maintaining an upright pelvis like a cup holding fluid within, allowing the lower back muscles to relax and flatten.

I have all my life had a lordosis (lower back curvature) I am now (when I remember) walking and sitting correcting my pelvic position. I'm hoping I will have started to maintain that position in everyday life. So I will ride with a level pelvis allowing gravity to correct my hip joints and legs position. Allowing my horses to use their hindquarters more freely.

Another Aha! moment while watching Listen to the Horse was the power of the mind in everyday life and with the horses. I always convince myself I not capable of being the best, fearing I will fail, being happy with second best, but wanting to be better for my horses.

Aha! I just caught myself telling myself this is boring and no one would want to read this. Shame! On me putting myself down I will continue regardless, instead of giving up.

Another Aha moment while watching Listen to the Horse was talking to the horses explaining and reassuring them in scary situations.

When I took my young horse Rocky to his first clinic away from the home, although he had many loading lessons he was anxious and reluctant to load. When loading him to go home I looked him in the eye and said "Come on we are going home". He picked himself up and walked on the float like a professional I was surprised and delighted. I am so looking forward to communicating more and seeing the responds.

Another Aha moment while watching Listen to the Horse allowing the horse to make decisions for himself and using this energy to one's own benefit. My young horses Rocky was going well at the trot but when asked for a canter transitions he would become anxious and toss his head.

After watching Listen to the Horse I trotted in a large paddock letting Rocky decide where we would go, back to the other horses of course. Then asked for a canter transition, it was smooth relaxed with no signs of concern Ya! It worked I tried again but this time I steered him away from the other horses, he was happy to oblige. We were working as a team making him a much more confident and willing partner.

Another Aha! moment while watching Listen to the Horse was don't have large expectations on yourself or your horses. I have always worked my horses slowly, but at times have my expectations have been way above myself and the horse's ability, which only just leads to frustration.

Now talking about frustrations, another Aha was "Take a break" stop go make a cup of tea when things get to hard and frustrating for you and the horse. I will now aim in for small positive steps that last forever and lots of cups of tea.

Lengthen your lower back

The Listening to the Horse movie inspired me to try to readjust my position in the saddle. I was fortunate enough to grow up with riding instruction that allowed me to develop basics in the Western and Hunter disciplines. Later, I became an eventer, and now I am enjoying learning more about my horse as I focus upon dressage.

Bouncing from one discipline to the other, I feel as if my position has experienced a little bit of whiplash. Unfortunately, for the most part, the instructors I have had tend to focus on whether horses and riders are getting the job done, no necessarily upon the rider's position. I've asked for assistance in my position and I've been told it's fine and I worry too much. I want better than "fine". I want to allow the horse to perform its best and to do everything I can to remain balanced and positioned so that I set the horse up for success.

Listening to the Horse gave me the idea to "lengthen my lower back". It was described as feeling as if I were slumping a little bit, but to think of it more as a lengthening. I've had the opportunity to try this with both of my horses and both responded beautifully to it!

Lengthening my lower back has made it easier for my horses to lift their backs and to keep their shoulders lifted too. This will revolutionize my riding! My horses were immediately more comfortable.

Since they were more comfortable, they will be more willing to maintain this postural frame that will enable them to utilize their muscles in a more even and correct manner. Therefore, by lengthening my back, my horse's will be able to move in such a way that their skeletons are protected, and their muscles provide the support necessary to assist their bodies in absorbing the impact of our movement.

Lengthening my lower back has also made it easier for me to feel the hoof falls of my horses. When a rider can feel the hoof falls, the aids can then be timed for optimum effect. This sets the horse up for greater success in understanding the communication from the rider. Now, when I ask for a longer stride in the walk, trot, or canter, I can feel the exact phase of the stride for maximum effect. Moreover, when I can feel the phases of the strides, I can also time the half halts with greater ease.

The small change of lengthening my lower back has enabled me to listen to my horses more closely. I am learning to feel when their muscles first begin to fatigue, which means I can tailor their work sessions so that they remain enjoyable and fun for both the horses and I. I am also able to time the aids with greater precision so that my horse has a better chance of understanding what it is that I am asking for. Now, when I ask for a change in the length of our strides, I don't have to hope I'm doing the right thing. Instead, I can focus and time my aids so that the response is natural and more likely correct.

These two, albeit early, results of lengthening my lower back have allowed me to turn down the volume of my aids and to pick up on what my horse is saying with more clarity. I am once again excited about every ride. I feel like new doors have been opened before me, and I feel like my horses and I can confidently step towards and through them with more harmonious communication.

Elaine Hildreth

Softness, patience and lightness

Listening to the Horse - A-Ha! But I don’t even have a horse! That's right, I don't even HAVE a horse. Wait - don't stop reading, this is relevant!

My name is Kelly and I am nearing 50 years old. I have wanted a horse my entire life. I have finally arrived in a place where having a horse is a reality.

I have been studying horsemanship and horse training for over a year now, sticking with one method of a particular trainer and using this method on my neighbor’s horse, (who graciously lets me play with one of her horses). I thought I was studying the "right" way when it came to training, but after watching the docu-series everything changed - BOOM - Mind Blown!

I had been working on backing the horse up on the ground because she is TERRIBLE at backing and very, very resistant with not much success. Meanwhile I start watching the series. Video after video I am noticing a recurring theme.

Each trainer emphasizes a soft, patient, light approach to with the horse. I decided to try getting her to back up with a soft approach to see what would happen. I honestly did not expect her to even move. She not only responded to this soft approach and began backing she was overall much more quiet.

The takeaway: It was not the horse that was terrible at backing up or resistant - it was me! This will change ALL of my future interactions with horses.

Now I have NEW Heroes thanks to your movie; Warwick Schiller, Steve Halfpenny, Karen Rohlf, just to name a few. Thanks to your series I learned that a much softer approach is best and these creatures are far more sensitive than I realized and it is exactly the kind of relationship I want with my future horse and companion!

So while I am currently not a horse owner, I hope to become one soon and thanks to your series I was able to look at things differently.

Kelly Rothwell.

Lessons learned

You ask us to describe an "aha" moment from the movie and how we've implemented the lesson learned. Well, for me, the "aha" was, "aha! I'm not so clueless after all!"

I have found enormous validation in the philosophy, opinions and explanations expressed by all the wise and wonderful horse people in the documentary. It has really bolstered my confidence in the approaches that I've been working on and learning for years.

Just to provide some context, I am what's referred to in these parts as a "back yard" horse person. For the past thirty or so years I have kept a few horses on my farm. One of the reasons I keep my horses with me on my own property is to try to avoid having to abide by other folks'
rules that I don't always agree with.

For most of these years I've had a busy career in IT and I've raised three daughters, so my riding has been somewhat sporadic.

From time to time I've had some riding lessons, but mostly I've just been learning on my own.

I've had to listen to some pretty opinionated people over the years telling me things like "you riding that horse yet?", "you need some draw reins on that horse", "you need a stronger bit", "you're too soft on that horse" and so on. You get the picture.

It's been stressful for me to withstand some of these commentaries, because most of these comments and opinions come from people who are way more experienced than I am, and I do respect that experience.

But I've also been lucky enough to have met some wonderful horse people who do, in fact, listen to their horses, and don't stand in judgement. And in recent years I've had a wonderful teacher who has helped me lot with listening to horses better.

And of course, my best teachers have been my horses.

I think the first time I actually listened to a horse was when I leased a mare for the summer when I was 19, and home for the summer from university. Thinking I was doing my best for this girl, I boarded her at a barn a few miles from my house and naively tried to put her into a standing stall. She balked at this, quite politely, but firmly, so aha! I switched her to pasture board, and she must have appreciated that I had listened to her as she obligingly let me walk up to her with a halter and piece of binder twine (I didn't have a lot of tack) and hop up on her bareback to go for a ride (oh for those days). Lesson learned.

I was incredibly lucky with the first horse I bought, years later, with human baby no. 3 only eight months old. It was only after his death at age 25, that I learned more about his breeding – he was a Raffles bred Arabian gelding and was quite the sweetest horse I've ever had. Early on, I tied him to a fence to brush him and aha! He told me quite clearly that he was not a fan of being tied up. So I just didn't tie him up. He didn't go anywhere, he stood quite happily with me and never wandered off. Lesson learned. (P.S. years later I did tie him up again and he was fine.)

Another lesson from Comar Olympian: he was better at negotiating trails than I was. He would stop and look for a while at a puddle or something across the trail, and once he'd decided it was okay, on he went. Aha! Leave it to the expert. Lesson learned.

I once rode out with someone who suggested I give him a whack, because he should go forward right away. Right. I know who I should have whacked.

A couple of years ago I bought a little Paso Fino who was for sale because his owner felt that he didn't like her. He wouldn't be caught but would obediently do whatever required of him once he'd been corralled. I felt that he would benefit from coming to live with me. He has taught me that time can be everything and that I don't need to listen to the people who tell me that he would benefit from regular work. Maybe, maybe not. But if he's not engaged and enjoying himself, what's the point? So we haven't done much yet, but his eye is softer, his ears aren't as pinned and he is a lot easier to catch. Aha! If he doesn't want to do something, I don't make him. He'll be ready at some point. Lesson learned.

If there's one horse that taught me that horses shouldn't be shut in stalls, it's my big horse, Dancer. He's the only horse baby I've ever had.

He is TB x Canadian, and he grew, and grew, and ended up 17.1 hh. He was way too big for me, and a handful (aha! No more backyard breeding) and I sold him (wouldn't do that now, sell him I mean). The best thing I did for him was to keep him barefoot and fancy free and unbacked till he was about 5. He went on to a career as a hunter jumper, which I've learned years later was not a good fit for him because of his size, and he learned how to crib because of an injury that kept him confined to a stall. He ended up with arthritis in his shoulder and providentially his owner gave him back to me.

The only time I ever ask him to go in a stall now is to get his grub, or to wait for the trimmer or the vet. Otherwise he does laps in there. He's no longer lame and is out and about and king of the hill at the age of 21. He's a lovely guy. I adore him and he's never leaving the farm again.

For the past few years I've been on the lookout for a smaller horse that I can ride comfortably, and who comes without physical or emotional baggage. I've had a couple of horses who didn't quite work out. There was Willow, the Arab x Welsh Cob who I'm pretty sure thought I was a bit dumb. He just got bored and liked to jump over the paddock fence and harass my old QH gelding. I do believe that there's a place for everyone and I ended up donating Willow to a therapeutic riding program. I had a sudden brainwave about this, aha! and now I've listened to some of the animal communicators, I'm wondering if Willow hadn't decided that he needed to tell me what to do. Last I heard, he was brilliant with the youngsters.

Then there was Holly, the rescued OTTB mare. Beautiful dark bay. She'd been through the mill and had at one point been rescued off a meat truck. She had many physical issues, including a history of ulcers and was a confirmed cribber. She came to me skinny and wormy. I think she figured out before I did that she and I were not a good fit as riding partners. I set about finding a new home for her and was delighted to be able to send her to live with a young couple who own and love one of her half brothers. She is loved.

Not sure what the “aha” might be there. Aha! Said my long suffering (non-horse person) husband. Giving away another horse you paid for. But I owe them.

And that brings me to Dawson.

Dawson is a young Kentucky Mountain horse, just coming up five years old this spring. He came to live with me last fall. Sometimes I think that I’ve gone bonkers, starting on a journey with such a young guy when I’m in my seventieth decade, but I’m also energized and excited about it. He is confident and not scared of much and is kind of like a giant Border Collie. He is interested in everything that’s going on and my biggest fear is that I’ll mess him up somehow. But my “aha” for him is: “aha! Everything I was planning to do with him is okay”, according to everything I heard in the movie.

He has been backed, but only lightly, last summer, with a bareback pad and halter. I’m planning only groundwork this year, next year, when he is 6, will be time enough to ride him.

I plan to ride him bitless. He has a very little mouth and I don’t want to stick metal in it. I think a rope halter with mecate rein will do the trick, or maybe one of the hackamores I saw in the movie.

We will do everything on the ground that I will expect him to do under saddle, but we'll go at his pace. I'm in no rush.

We will train him in classical dressage, because although he's a gaited breed, and gaited horses are often trained to go high-headed and hollow backed, I want him to learn self carriage and true collection so he can be sound in his mind and body for years to come.

I'm going to get professional help with his training because I'm not confident enough in my own ability to execute although I know in theory what I'm after. I just have to find someone who agrees with all the above. I'm sure I will.

This is my promise to this young horse. Thank you.

Inspiration with Jim, Jeff and Lester

In the episode featuring Bodywork featuring Jim Masterson I learned about the Bladder Meridian Technique.

I have seen and heard of equine massage, but I had not learned any techniques or watched a demonstration of it. After watching Mr. Masterson twice, and being very impressed by the horse's calmed reaction and how Jim Masterson addressed the issues of eye blinking, I went out to try the Bladder Meridian Technique on my very timid, very untrusting, always bracing mustang.

When I first got him he would not trust me to stand near him while he ate. He would always wait until I left. Thankfully, we have moved passed that and he will eat in my presence now.

Without halter I went down both his left and right side four times while he had his feedbag in front of him. He was curious and stopped eating and backed up while I did the technique. He was weary at first, but the more I did it, the more he softened. He started to lower his head, lick his lips, and chew.

My biggest goal was to help him un-brace his neck as that is what he immediately does whenever anyone approaches him – getting ready for flight. I was elated to have him lowering his neck as I rubbed in the spots where his eyes blinked.

After I finished I was hoping he would come and ask for more massaging, but he went back to eating. But, I know he enjoyed it and softened and that was fantastic for him.

I also learned a lot from Jeff Sanders. He didn't speak a lot about it, but he spoke some about a horse with what we call a sway back. My mustang has a sway back and I can tell from his movements that it is because of his bad posture. I learned from Jeff Sanders that this bad posture is because Prior doesn't bring his hind end under him and pulls his body too much with his front end. He's lacking in his stomach muscles and just plain learning how to carry himself in a more collected and correct way.

Lester Buckley also touched on this in his story about riding a young mare gathering cattle – damaging the mare's back because of a not perfectly fitting saddle, riding her too long, and not learning to post during the trot. I wonder if this has happened to my mustang.

I've only owned him 2 going on 3 years. He's 17 years old and has had 6 different owners. I have no idea how they rode him, but perhaps they used a poor fitting saddle, or rode him too long and too hard one day, or maybe they did not or do not post during the trot. Maybe they've done all three things.

To remedy his sway back I have put in several poles he must walk over to get to his water trough. As the weather here improves I plan to ride him and lunge him over small jumps that will hopefully strengthen his core so that his posture may improve.

Jeff Sanders also had a really great demonstration and explanation about bits. I watched this section twice as well.

I now know I need to check out my horse's mouth size and tongue size so that I can purchase a bit that will fit each horse the way it should without putting restriction or undue pressure on their tongue and bars. I'd really like to try a hackamore. Especially as Jeff Sanders says it can deliver the signal and communication just as well as a bit.

Jeff Sanders also spoke about the rider position in relation to the ribcage, specifically the rib numbers, of the horse. I got a good idea of where the rider really needs to sit, which I had not paid as much attention to as I very much should. That was very, very interesting. Once the weather warms up here and I can ride outside I'm definitely planning to look at my saddles on my horses.

I have an Australian saddle I love a lot, but it really tends to put you in a rocking chair type of position and I wonder if it's positioning me wrong on the horse's back – and hurting my horse. If so, I'll have to revisit changing saddles. Thank you for putting this movie together.

Q. Sondeno

Final thoughts from Elaine

I want to thank everyone who watched the movie and sent in a story for consideration. I loved all of these stories, and I was in tears more than once reading them! Unfortunately it wasn't possible to include all of the stories in one book, but I hope you have enjoyed the stories that were chosen.

These stories were based on experiences people had after watching the award-winning documentary 'Listening to the Horse'.

If you haven't yet seen the documentary, or if you'd like to would enjoy watching it again, you can get a free ticket to enjoy episode 1 of this seven part docu-series at: www.listentothehorse.com

I hope that you enjoyed the wonderful stories in this book.

Elaine Heney

www.greyponyfilms.com

ONLINE HORSE TRAINING COURSES

Printed in Great Britain
by Amazon

68381249R00078